Mathematics Assessment

Cases and Discussion Questions

FOR GRADES K–5

CLASSROOM ASSESSMENT
FOR SCHOOL MATHEMATICS

Editor

William S. Bush

Case Editors

William S. Bush

Lise Dworkin

Deborah Bryant Spencer

K–12 SERIES ■

Mathematics Assessment

Cases and Discussion Questions

FOR GRADES K–5

NATIONAL COUNCIL
OF TEACHERS OF
MATHEMATICS
RESTON, VIRGINIA

NCTM

Library of Congress Cataloging-in-Publication Data

Mathematics assessment : cases and discussion questions for grades K–5 / editor
William S. Bush.
    p. cm. — (Classroom assessment for school mathematics K–12 series)
  Includes bibliographical references and index.
  ISBN 0-87353-497-2
  1. Mathematics—Study and teaching (Primary)—United States—Evaluation. 2.
Mathematics—Study and teaching (Elementary)—United States—Evaluation. 3.
Mathematical ability—Testing. I. Bush, William S. II. Series. Classroom assessment for
school mathematics K–12.

QA135.5 .M36774 2001
372.7'0973—dc21
                                       2001018008

Table of Contents

Acknowledgments vi

Letter to Readers vii

Introduction 2

CHAPTER 1: CASES ABOUT USING NEW ASSESSMENT APPROACHES   6

    The Power of the Blank Page 6

    On-the-Job Learning 12

    How Do I Assess Thee? Let Me Count the Ways 14

    Primary Portfolios 19

    When the Wrong Way Works 24

CHAPTER 2: CASES ABOUT SCORING ASSESSMENT   26

    A Team Approach 26

    If They Only Knew Michael 28

    Students as Assessors 33

CHAPTER 3: CASES ABOUT USING ASSESSMENT RESULTS   38

    The New Student 38

    Melanie's Place-Value Understanding 41

    A Rubric Solves My Problem 47

    Show and Tell 53

    Student-Led Conferences 59

CHAPTER 4: FACILITATOR GUIDELINES AND NOTES   62

    Guidelines for Facilitating Cases 62

    Notes for "The Power of the Blank Page" 66

    Notes for "On-the-Job Learning" 68

    Notes for "How Do I Assess Thee? Let Me Count the Ways ..." . . . 70

    Notes for "Primary Portfolios" 72

    Notes for "When the Wrong Way Works" 75

    Notes for "A Team Approach" 77

    Notes for "If They Only Knew Michael" 79

    Notes for "Students as Assessors" 82

    Notes for "The New Student" 85

    Notes for "Melanie's Place-Value Understanding" 87

    Notes for "A Rubric Solves My Problem" 90

    Notes for "Show and Tell" 92

    Notes for "Student-Led Conferences" 94

Bibliography 98

Index 101

ACKNOWLEDGMENTS

We wish to thank the following teachers for contributing cases to this book. Without their willingness to share part of their teaching lives with us, this book would not have been possible.

Brenda Brooks	Carol Midgett
Tammy Collum	Lori Murakami
Rosalyn Haberkern	Donna Redwine
Rhona Harkness	Sandy Silverman
Barbara Hutton	Sheila Stearns
Tad Johnson	Lois Williams

We wish to thank Nola Aitken of the University of Lethbridge, who encouraged teachers in her classes to submit stories about their assessment experiences. We also wish to thank Lise Dworkin of the San Francisco Unified School District for working with teachers to write assessment cases. Her initial editing of these cases made our work easier.

In addtion, we would like to thank Carne Barnett of WestEd, who served as a consultant to this project from the outset. Her expertise in helping teachers write cases, in helping us edit cases, and in helping us think about how to use cases in professional development activities proved invaluable.

Finally, we wish to thank Katherine Merseth, Joan Karp, and Carolyn Ronchinsky of the Harvard Mathematics Case Development Project for sharing their expertise in case writing. Their valuable advice helped us in shaping cases that would be useful to teachers.

THE ASSESSMENT ADDENDA TASK FORCE

William S. Bush, *Chair*

Charles Allen

Florence Glanfield

Anja S. Greer

Steve Leinwand

Jean Kerr Stenmark

Dear Reader,

The National Council of Teachers of Mathematics asked our task force to create an Addenda Series to support the Assessment Standards for School Mathematics. This book, one of six books in the series, provides descriptions of real activities, students, and teachers in assessment situations in grades K–5 classrooms. It also includes reflective questions to encourage discussion about important issues in assessment. Four Practical Handbooks for teachers in grades K–2, 3–5, 6–8, and 9–12 contain practical examples and ideas from teachers who have been successful with assessment. Another book presents assessment cases from grades 6–12 classrooms.

The Assessment Standards tells us that classroom assessment should—

- provide a rich variety of mathematical topics and problem situations;
- give students opportunities to investigate problems in many ways;
- question and listen to students;
- look for evidence of learning from many sources;
- expect students to use concepts and procedures effectively in solving problems.

Our collection of examples, reflections, explanations, and tips are intended to help all of us explore the role of assessment in reshaping mathematics teaching and learning. We know that assessment, from simple observations to standardized tests, has always affected what we do in the classroom. We looked for examples that help us do a better job and that allow us to become clearer about what we really want students to learn.

We also know that classrooms and schools are complex places. Changing assessment practices in nonsupportive environments is challenging at best. We will share the experiences and stories of teachers who have had some success. We will also share the stories of teachers who have struggled with assessment.

Many people contributed to this effort. Classroom teachers and teacher educators have shared their assessment stories in this book to encourage us to reflect on our assessment practices and on our beliefs about assessment, teaching, and learning.

This book, Cases and Discussion Questions for Grades K–5, is divided into five sections. The first, "Introduction," explains what cases are, what their purposes are, and what advantages they hold as a professional development tool. The next three sections include thirteen cases that share the assessment stories of mathematics teachers across the continent. The last section, "Facilitator Guidelines and Notes," offers helpful hints to lead groups of teachers in discussions about the cases. It also includes specific notes and suggestions for facilitating each case. Finally, we have provided a bibliography for further reading and an index at the end to help you locate topics of greatest interest to you.

We hope you will find many uses for this book. Enjoy!

—The Assessment Addenda Task Force

Mathematics Assessment: Cases and Discussion Questions for Grades K–5

Introduction

The National Council of Teachers of Mathematics provides a vision of classroom assessment that will enable us to assess the full mathematics power of our students. This vision is reflected through recommendations in the Evaluation section of the *Curriculum and Evaluation Standards for School Mathematics* (1989), through the *Assessment Standards for School Mathematics* (1995), and through the *Principles and Standards for School Mathematics* (2000).

The *Assessment Standards* shares six standards to guide us:

Standard 1: Assessment should reflect the mathematics that all students need to know and be able to do.

Standard 2: Assessment should enhance mathematics learning.

Standard 3: Assessment should promote equity.

Standard 4: Assessment should be an open process.

Standard 5: Assessment should promote valid inferences about mathematics learning.

Standard 6: Assessment should be a coherent process.

Meeting these standards might require significant changes in our assessment practices. **Figure A** outlines a set of shifts in practices that must occur if we are to meet these standards for classroom assessment.

FIG. A

MAJOR SHIFTS IN ASSESSMENT PRACTICE (from National Council of Teachers of Mathematics [NCTM] 1995, p. 83)

TOWARD	AWAY FROM
Assessing students' full mathematical power	Assessing only students' knowledge of specific facts and isolated skills
Comparing students' performance with established criteria	Comparing students' performance with that of other students
Giving support to teachers and credence to their informed judgment	Designing "teacher-proof" assessment systems
Making the assessment process public, participatory, and dynamic	Making the assessment process secret, exclusive, and fixed
Giving students multiple opportunities to demonstrate their full mathematical power	Restricting students to a single way of demonstrating their mathematical knowledge
Developing a shared vision of what to assess and how to do it	Developing assessment by oneself
Using assessment results to ensure that all students have the opportunity to achieve their potential	Using assessment to filter and select students out of the opportunities to learn mathematics
Aligning assessment with curriculum and instruction	Treating assessment as independent of curriculum or instruction
Basing inferences on multiple sources of evidence	Basing inferences on restricted or single sources of evidence
Viewing students as active participants in the assessment process	Viewing students as the objects of assessment
Regarding assessment as continual and recursive	Regarding assessment as sporadic and conclusive
Holding all concerned with mathematics learning accountable for assessment results	Holding only a few accountable for assessment results

Introduction

Making important shifts in assessment practice is a difficult task. The result, however, is a clearer picture of what our students know about mathematics, what they can do with mathematics, and of how they think mathematically. Using a variety of valid, reliable assessment tools can help us understand and ultimately communicate to others the mathematics power our students hold.

We have found that one of the best ways to learn about assessment and make changes in practices is through work with other teachers. Listening to teachers talk about their experiences, watching other teachers at work, and working beside colleagues show us ways to learn new approaches. By doing so, we are often challenged to question some of the practices we or other teachers have used over the years.

For these reasons, NCTM developed *Mathematics Assessment: Cases and Discussion Questions for Grades K–5* as a professional development tool both for teachers who want to change their assessment practices and for teachers who have struggled with changes over the years. This book provides a glimpse into the assessment experiences of elementary school teachers of mathematics around the continent. Through these cases, we hope that you will reflect on your own assessment practices and analyze your beliefs about assessment, teaching, and learning. In discussing these cases with others, we hope that you will learn strategies to improve your classroom assessment practices.

WHAT ARE THE CASES ABOUT ASSESSMENT?

The cases in this book are stories written by mathematics teachers or other educators describing experiences with classroom assessment. They were designed to raise issues and pose dilemmas about assessment.

WHAT ARE THE PURPOSES OF CASES ABOUT ASSESSMENT?

These cases are professional development tools designed to—

- ■ stimulate reflection about assessment practices;
- ■ explore issues about classroom assessment;
- ■ encourage the examination of beliefs about classroom assessment.

As a professional development tool, they have several advantages:

- ■ They allow us to analyze teaching and assessment practices carefully and respectfully.
- ■ They allow us to analyze and solve teaching problems collaboratively.
- ■ They allow us to bring our own meanings and experiences to each problem or dilemma.
- ■ They model classroom teaching where students must analyze and solve problems on their own.
- ■ They help us build a repertoire of strategies for resolving difficult classroom dilemmas.
- ■ They expose us to many different points of view about assessment.

Introduction

HOW DO I USE THIS BOOK?

This book is intended to be used as a professional development tool for mathematics teachers in grades K–5. It is appropriate for beginning teachers as well as teachers with experience—including those who have tried many different types of classroom assessment. We believe that all of us can learn from the discussions sparked by the dilemmas presented in these cases.

We suggest that the cases be read and discussed in groups. The assessment cases here can be used as a professional development experience in themselves, or they may be used to supplement professional development workshops that focus on assessment strategies.

The assessment cases may also be used in teacher preparation courses to help prospective teachers learn about mathematics assessment and the issues that surround it. Student teachers and their cooperating teachers may read and discuss the cases as a means to understand each other's assessment practices and beliefs.

Finally, the cases can be used for individual professional growth. By simply sitting down and reading the cases alone, teachers can gain insight into their assessment practices. If the cases are used in this manner, however, we recommend that the facilitator notes be read along with the cases to stimulate reflection about a wide range of issues.

Introduction

WHERE CAN I FIND OTHER CASES ABOUT MATHEMATICS ASSESSMENT?

Fractions, Decimals, Ratios, & Percents: Hard to Learn and Hard to Teach, by Carne Barnett, Donna Goldenstein, and Babette Jackson, offers twenty-nine cases written about learning and teaching rational numbers. Many of these cases focus on important issues about classroom assessment. A facilitator guide to assist in leading discussions about the cases is sold separately.

Developing Mathematical Ideas—Number and Operations: Building a System of Tens, by Deborah Shifter, Virginia Bastable, and Susan Jo Russell, includes twenty-eight written cases focused on students' learning of place value. Although these cases focus on instructional issues and student thinking, many cases also address important issues of assessment. With this volume, one can purchase a facilitator guide to help stimulate discussions about the cases.

Developing Mathematical Ideas—Making Meaning for Operations, by Deborah Shifter, Virginia Bastable, and Susan Jo Russell, includes twenty-eight written cases focused on students' learning of addition, subtraction, multiplication, and division. Although these cases focus on instructional issues and students' thinking, many also address important issues of assessment. With the volume, one can purchase a facilitator guide to help stimulate discussions about the cases.

Casebook of School Reform, edited by Barbara Miller and Ilene Kantrov, offers cases about school reform. Some cases focus on mathematics and assessment.

Mathematics Assessment: A Video Library, K–12 was produced by the Educational Programming Group of the WGBH Educational Foundation. It includes six videotaped cases, complete with classroom action followed by teacher reflection. It comes with a guidebook to assist with using the videos in professional development experiences.

Using Assessment to Reshape Teaching: A Casebook for Mathematics Teachers and Teacher Educators, edited by Sandra Wilcox and Perry Lanier, offers additional cases about assessment and its effect on instruction.

<table>
<tr><td>

Chapter 1

</td><td>

Cases about Using New Assessment Approaches

</td></tr>
</table>

The Power of the Blank Page

It was March, time for spring cleaning in my classroom. I left a tall stack of booklets on the edge of the counter near the classroom library. The booklets were stapled copier paper, completely blank except for one single number written at the top of each page. I originally intended to use them as counting booklets, thought better of the idea, and stashed them away just in case I thought of another use.

Three of my first graders discovered the booklets and asked if they could have them for the class. "What will you do with them?" I asked.

They responded excitedly, "We could do plus and subtract."

"We could draw pictures that make the right number."

"I would do hard math, and when I was finished with it, I would give it to the people that have hard problems that they don't know."

I asked what they would say to the class about the number 1 written at the top of the first page. Chris enthusiastically offered, "I was thinking the math problems. Like $1 + 16 = 17$. Then minus the 16 would make it go to 1. (See **fig. 1.1**.) I think we should write on it the things that make 1. On the 3 page, I'd make some 3s here like $6 - 3 = 3$."

FIG. 1.1

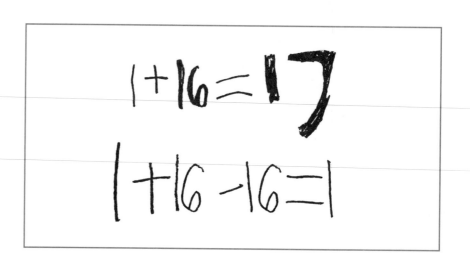

Flipping back to page 1, he continued, "OK, want me to show that to you on the paper?" He wrote $6 - 5 = 1$. He told me, "I've been thinking it all the time. I just started from $3 - 2$, $4 - 3$, $5 - 4$, $6 - 5$. I just did it all the way."

Joan suggested, "When you take away, you do something—like if I write something, like a number, it has to equal 1. And tell the kids that. They should do it because it'll learn them how to plus and subtract."

The children presented their ideas to the class, and these are some of the results.

The Power of the Blank Page

Joan

Joan had taken her number booklet, attached it to a clipboard, and positioned herself comfortably on the pillows in the class library area. She worked very quietly during the morning, sitting next to her friends but choosing to work independently.

She brought her booklet to me and announced, "This is a really hard one— look at all the zeros," as she pointed to the equation $0 + 0 + 0 + 0 + 2 - 1 = 1$. "I know how to make it really long." A closer look at her work showed her understanding that 1 can be obtained by subtracting one less than any given quantity. (See **fig. 1.2**.)

FIG. 1.2

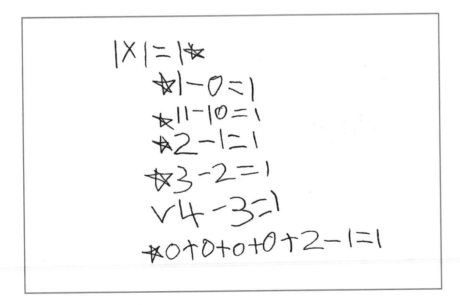

Joan cleverly incorporated multiplication, addition, and subtraction in her equations. She knew $9 \times 9 = 81$ and then knew how to subtract the number that is one less (80) in order to equal 1.

"Can you tell me about this part?" I asked, pointing to 9×9. (See **fig. 1.3**.)

"I just know 9×9 is 81.... My brother told me. Times is kind of hard, but it's easy for me ... like 2×3, you just know it."

I asked Joan if she could draw me a picture of 2×3. Her response was, "You just know it ... you just have 3 blocks and 3 blocks ... it doesn't matter how big they are." She then showed me how to use the calculator to figure out multiplication facts that she hadn't memorized. "It's easy to make 1. Just 8×7 [using the calculator] is 56, take away 55 to make 1...." And she ended our discussion by telling me about several other possibilities.

FIG. 1.3

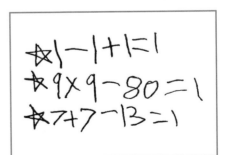

The Power of the Blank Page

Frank

Frank quickly gathered his number booklet, a fistful of colored pencils, and a calculator. As he dashed past me to a table, he said, "Of course, I'm going to do the hard math," referring to division. Frank was a very confident student who often struggled with his mathematics but always persevered.

Earlier in the week, he had asked his fifth-grade buddy to teach him how to do that hard mathematics, making a sketch that looked like long division. His buddy showed him how to use a calculator to solve simple division problems. (See **fig. 1.4**.) Frank's paper was covered with "calculator number" equations, showing that he knew the technique that any number divided by itself equaled 1. However, neither his work nor his discussions demonstrated real understanding of the larger concept of division.

FIG. 1.4

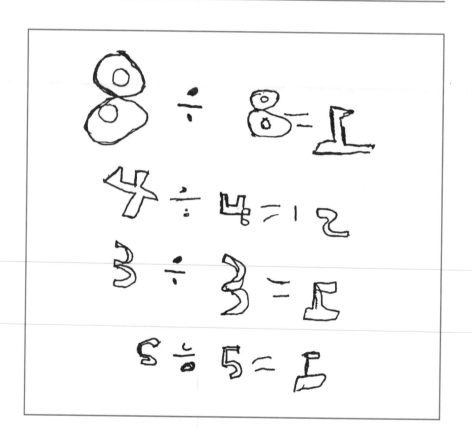

The Power of the Blank Page

When I asked Frank to think of other ways to make 1, he could not respond immediately and instead went back to the table to work. Several minutes later he returned with 8 – 8 = 1 written on his paper in "plain numbers." During our discussion, it was clear that he was confused that the pattern he had discovered worked for division but not for subtraction. He worked quite a while longer to generate two correct subtraction problems. (See **fig. 1.5**.)

FIG. 1.5

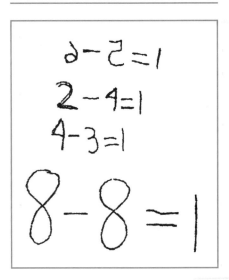

Alisha

Giant crocodile tears dripped down her cheeks as Alisha asked, "Do I have to use numbers? I just like letters." Alisha was a very verbal student, writing book after book filled with invented spelling and large expressive pictures. She felt very competent expressing herself verbally and was equally as uncomfortable in the world of numbers.

Alisha reluctantly picked up her number booklet, searched out just the right crayons and marking pens, and sat very close to her best friend. Together they generated a variety of equations to equal 4. (See **fig. 1.6**.)

FIG. 1.6

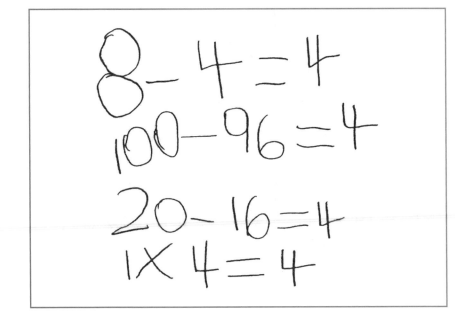

When I asked Alisha to explain her work, she replied, "I don't like this." Alisha helped her friend record the work, but she did not create it or seem to understand it.

"Can't I just write something?" she lamented. I asked her what she would like to write, and she wrote her friend's name, "Francesca."

"How can we use this to show 4?" I asked. She took her paper and wrote one number under each letter. (See **fig. 1.7**.)

FIG. 1.7

The Power of the Blank Page

"But that's not 4," she sighed.

"What else could you do?" I asked. She added "+ Alisha." When I asked if that made 4, she wrote the numbers under her own name. (See **fig. 1.8**.)

FIG. 1.8

Again I asked gently, "Does that make 4?" At this point, she realized that she had too many letters and needed to take some away. She pointed to F and wrote "–F," pointed to R and wrote "–R." She pointed and wrote letters until all of them were used from "Francesca."

"Does that make 4?" She counted all the letters written so far on the page and decided there were still too many. She pointed to the last A in her name, wrote "–A," and then counted all the letters again. She pointed to the H in her name, wrote "H," and then counted all the letters again. She was satisfied that she had 4. (See **fig. 1.9**.)

FIG. 1.9

CHAPTER *1*

The Power of the Blank Page

Next, she decided to use the name of another friend, Nancy. This time she wrote "Nancy + Alisha" in one quick phrase. She counted, realized she had too much, and took away "Alisha" as one entire unit. She was able to work with entire chunks of letters instead of having to count one by one. She counted again, then subtracted the Y from the end of Nancy's name. (See **fig. 1.10**.)

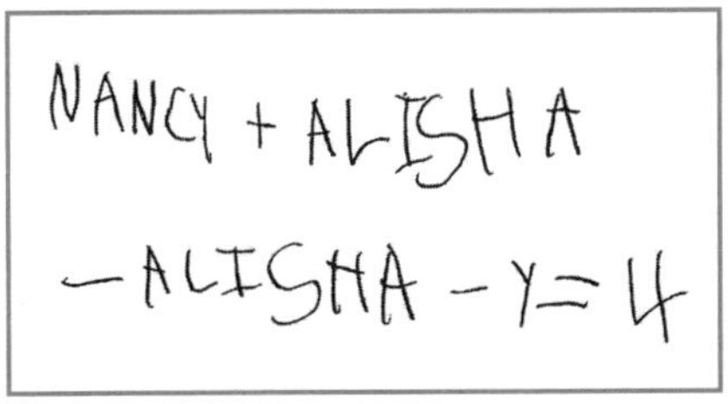

"Could you take away the N instead?" I asked. "No, that's the number 1—you have to keep that one." When I pushed her to record one more way to equal 4, she quickly and confidently strung together four letter A's representing her own name. (See **fig. 1.11**.)

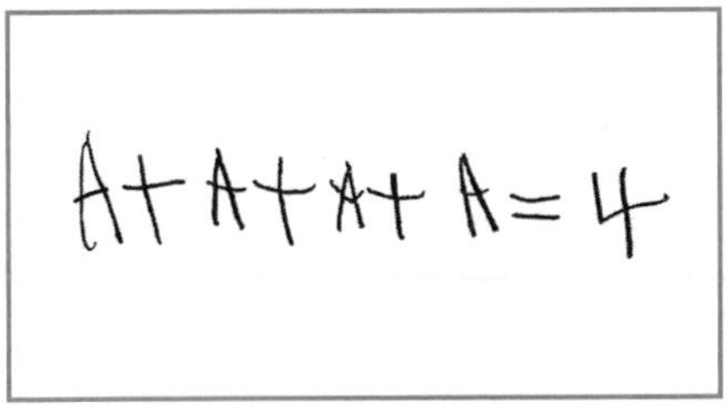

MORE QUESTIONS THAN ANSWERS

The number booklet activity, or as the children called it, "The How to Make One Books," came from the children themselves. These children made decisions about classroom events throughout the year, and they had many prior experiences with creating equations for everyday mathematical situations. I had no idea, however, that their work would display such unique mathematical thinking.

As this activity came to an end, I found myself filled with questions. I wondered about my students. Was it a problem that Joan was using multiplication without understanding it? How can I take advantage of Frank's willingness to explore patterns? Would Alisha's newfound confidence transfer to her next mathematical project? I wondered whether my regular mathematics instruction would have revealed the same depth of students' mathematical thinking that this simple activity did. Did I really understand what my students knew about numbers and operations? How might I more systematically gather this kind of evidence about my students' understanding of numbers?

FIG. 1.10

$$\text{NANCY} + \text{ALISHA}$$
$$-\text{ALISHA} - Y = 4$$

FIG. 1.11

$$A + A + A + A = 4$$

On-the-Job Learning

A few years ago I attended a summer workshop on assessment. The presenter emphasized the importance of recording assessment notes on students so that teachers could document students' learning to aid in future lesson planning. I could see the value of this type of assessment, but since I had not yet tried it in my own first-grade classroom, I wanted to know the logistics. For example, how could I keep detailed notes on twenty-four children? I quickly learned that even though the presenter had some good ideas on how to accomplish such a task, I would need help in figuring out how to accomplish this task "on the job." I left the workshop accepting the challenge but wondering how to start.

I knew that there were a certain number of students, a certain amount of time, and a certain quality of notes that had to be obtained in order to assure success with this type of assessment. I needed a plan to document my students' learning so that I could share accurate information with parents and better shape my own teaching.

KEEPING NOTES

When I first began keeping observation notes on students, my goal was to spend quality time with a number of students each day. I simply tried to take notes on what I heard. Determined to talk to as many students as possible, I raced around my classroom every day. I quickly learned that most of my time was devoted to watching the clock and worrying that I would not get to enough students. "Where was my next student located in the room?" "How many more students did I need to talk to?" Before long, I began to question the effectiveness of this weary schedule. My attempts at record keeping had left me exhausted and unfulfilled. I had set an all-too-hopeful schedule for assessing students and had not obtained the benefits I had wanted.

I sat down one day and thought through my plan. "Could I come up with something better?" "Why was I keeping records in the first place?" After much thought, I decided that my task was to determine the level of my students' understanding. Most important, I wanted to use this information to plan what to do next in my lesson.

OBSERVING STUDENTS

First, I decided to make the schedule more manageable by reducing the number of students I would assess each day. I would focus more on spending quality time with fewer students. I also needed a tool for recording and organizing all the information I gathered. I chose a grid as my recording sheet. The grid looked like a monthly calendar with each student's name written in a box. I used a highlighter to mark the students that I would observe or talk to that day. Being able to see all the students' names on a sheet helped me organize the process. I knew at a glance which students to observe.

Moreover, I developed my own "shorthand" in an effort to save time. SC stood for "self-corrected" and SO followed by a word meant that a student had been successful sounding out that word while reading. For mathematics, TTH and a check meant that a student was successful telling time to the hour after seeing several examples. The more I used my new system, the better I became with my shorthand and capturing what students were thinking.

CHAPTER *1*

On-the-Job Learning

With clipboard in hand and calendar grid highlighted with the five or six children I would assess that day, I was ready to take notes. The system worked better than I had expected. The note-taking was more manageable for smaller numbers of students each day. Sometimes, I simply listened to students and recorded what I heard in their conversation that might reflect their thinking. I found that students explained best when they worked together in groups. Their thinking became "public" because they had to defend their thinking to their peers or help peers by teaching them something. At other times, I was more active in questioning students about their thinking: While a student played a mathematics game with a partner, I would ask questions about an answer and the strategies for obtaining the answer. The longer I spent with a student, the more probing my questions became. I might also sit with a student who was completing a mathematics worksheet or working on the Problem of the Day and ask questions about the process for finding an answer. Often I found myself saying to a student, "I need you to talk out loud while you solve this problem so I can hear what you are thinking."

Of course, the students wondered what I wrote on my clipboard and why I asked them questions. I eventually explained to the whole class that I was recording their good work so I could tell their parents. This explanation seemed to satisfy them, and it was the truth. However, another task for me was to work on the students' comfort level with my note-taking. Some students were not always comfortable with my requests for explanations and my questions and often seemed uneasy when I wrote on my grid after their comments.

FACING CHALLENGES

Despite my satisfaction with my note-taking strategy, I continue to face a persistent challenge. Sometimes I walk by a student who is doing something that I think ought to be documented, but then I realize that he or she is not on my list for observation that day. There's a lot of learning taking place all over the classroom that I am not capturing. Those learning moments are like windows into the students' learning, and they provide a direction for me as a teacher to follow. How can I capture this important information and still keep the system manageable and ensure that I take notes on all my students?

Finally, I struggle with what to do with all the information that I have collected. It is useful to me, and I often incorporate what I've learned about students' thinking into my lesson planning. Sometimes I even make midcourse corrections during class. I'd like to take the information further, however, and use it in conferences with parents. Eventually I want to use it in conferences with my students. My calendar grid helps me get snapshots of my whole class, but how can I best use all this information I've gathered?

How Do I Assess Thee?
Let Me Count the Ways ...

FIG. 1.12

POW #3
I. PROBLEM STATEMENT
Restate the problem in your own words, giving only the necessary information. Explain clearly enough so that someone picking up your paper could understand exactly what you were asked to do. Make it CLEAR, CONCISE, and CORRECT.
II. PROCESS
Explain clearly how you went about solving the problem. Use diagrams, pictures, charts, and so on to help you illustrate your strategy. Explain what you did first and why you did that; what you did next and why. Continue to do this for each step you did.
III. LEARNING
What did you learn about mathematics from this problem? About yourself? Was the problem too easy, too difficult, or just right? Why?
IV. CONCLUSION
What answer did you get? What makes you think it is the correct solution? Could there be other correct answers? Explain why.
▪ **BONUS STAR**
Earn a bonus star by finding and describing another way to solve the problem or by finding another answer for the problem.

"How do you assess your students' mathematical understanding?" queried my university mathematics instructor. "How can you tell what your students really know about the mathematical concepts you teach them?" These questions caused me to reflect on my own teaching practices and, in particular, the way that I made decisions about my students' abilities.

I am a fourth- and fifth-grade bilingual teacher working in an urban public school. After seventeen years as a teacher, I believe I have studied and put into practice much of what is advocated in the NCTM *Curriculum and Evaluation Standards for School Mathematics* (National Council of Teachers of Mathematics [NCTM] 1989). Though I was well aware of many different assessment tools for mathematics and how they could guide instruction, I did not yet have a comprehensive method to assess my students. Problems of the Week (POWs), journals, investigations, on-demand tasks, performance assessment—I wanted to do it all. In the past, I relied heavily on weekly POWs, occasional tests, and observations. I used other assessment tools and had students participate in longer explorations and activities, but I never established a consistent, varied formal assessment program in my classroom.

A DIFFERENT YEAR

I intended to make this year different. I team taught with another teacher and was responsible for assessing the mathematical abilities and needs of sixty-three fourth- and fifth-grade students. I knew I had to find a way to keep track of each student's learning. I was determined to use a variety of assessment tools this time, and I was excited by the prospect of finally having an organized assessment program in place. I still planned to follow my yearlong math curriculum, but I planned to vary my assessments to ensure that I covered different aspects of students' learning. Each month, I planned to use four types of assessment, a different one for each week. When teaching the number strand, for example, I decided to assign POWs for the first week. (See fig. **1.12**.)

FIG. 1.12 (Continued)

Common Cents

Each of the three rows and three columns of coins here contains the same amount of money. That's because there may be a second coin under any or all of the coins you see. No stack contains more than two coins, and no stack contains two coins of the same denomination. How much money is in each row and column, and how is it distributed?

CHAPTER *1*

How Do I Assess Thee?
Let Me Count the Ways …

During the second week, I decided to use performance tasks like having students create a five-step number sentence, prove its correct solution to a small group, or solve another student's number sentence during a mental mathematics performance assessment. (See **fig. 1.13**.)

FIG. 1.13

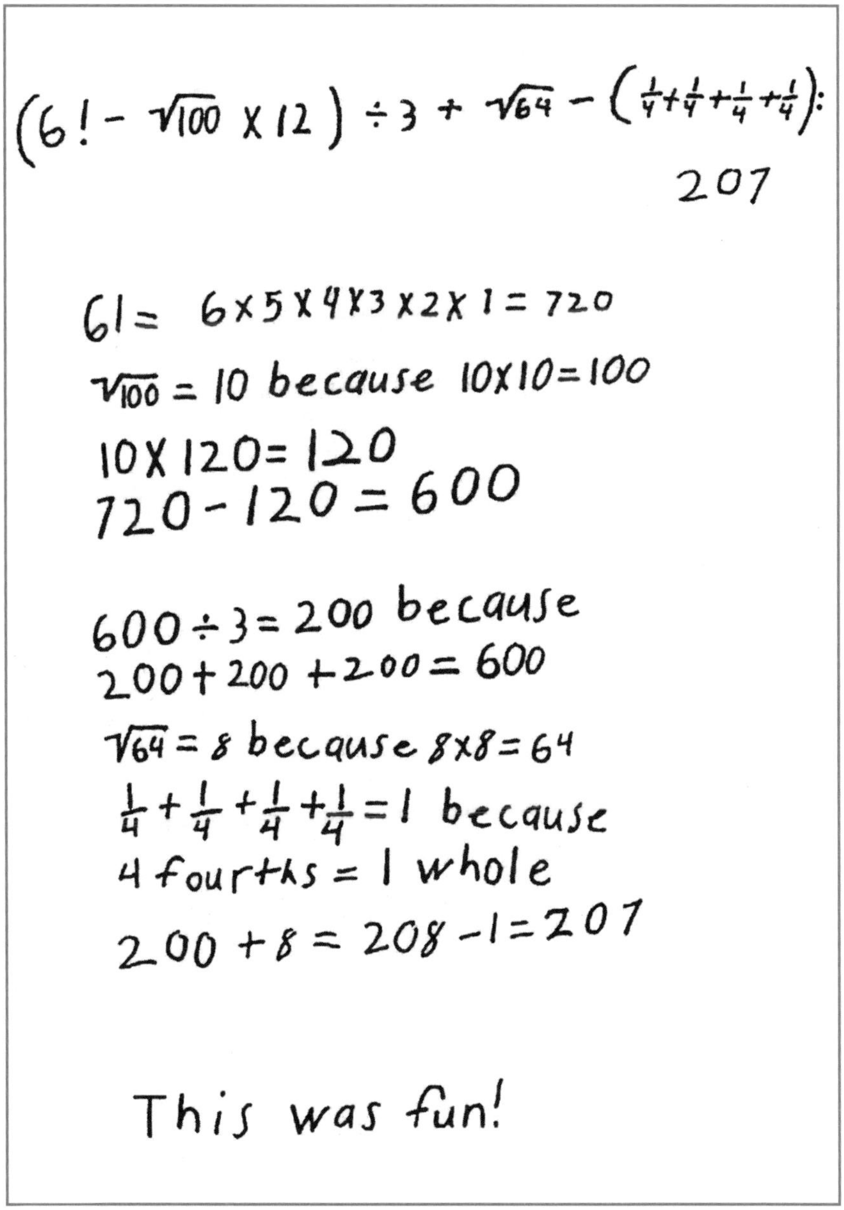

$$\left(6! - \sqrt{100} \times 12\right) \div 3 + \sqrt{64} - \left(\tfrac{1}{4}+\tfrac{1}{4}+\tfrac{1}{4}+\tfrac{1}{4}\right):$$

207

$6! = 6 \times 5 \times 4 \times 3 \times 2 \times 1 = 720$

$\sqrt{100} = 10$ because $10 \times 10 = 100$

$10 \times 120 = 120$
$720 - 120 = 600$

$600 \div 3 = 200$ because
$200 + 200 + 200 = 600$
$\sqrt{64} = 8$ because $8 \times 8 = 64$
$\tfrac{1}{4} + \tfrac{1}{4} + \tfrac{1}{4} + \tfrac{1}{4} = 1$ because
4 fourths = 1 whole
$200 + 8 = 208 - 1 = 207$

This was fun!

How Do I Assess Thee?
Let Me Count the Ways ...

During the third week, I planned to assign investigations to explore mathematics topics like the Fibonacci sequence. During the fourth week, I planned to give quizzes, asking students to solve number sentences such as $7 \times 8 = ?$, to explain what it means, to draw a picture to illustrate the number sentence, or to write a related story problem. (See **fig. 1.14**.)

FIG. 1.14

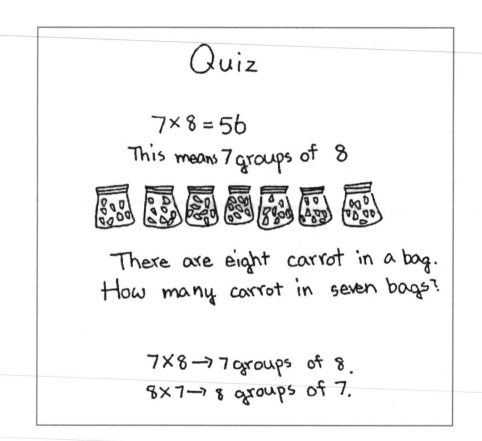

In addition, at the end of each strand unit, I wanted to ask students to write summaries of the activities or lessons, to explain what they learned from them, and to share their thoughts and ideas about the mathematics content.

How Do I Assess Thee?
Let Me Count the Ways ...

My classes always have limited (LEP) or non-English (NEP) proficient students. Despite my ability to translate and communicate with them in their language, it has been a difficult task to ensure that they completely understand everything we do in class. POWs are especially difficult for them because all our class discussions about strategies and students' thinking are conducted in English. It is impossible for me or peer translators to provide direct translations of every thought, inquiry, or idea when the discussions become involved. I often get caught up in the action, asking questions, listening to explanations, challenging students to justify their thinking, then feeling guilty that I have not always checked to ensure that my LEP and NEP students understand everything we have discussed.

This year would be different. This time I had several different assessment tools to use to document my students' understanding and performance, and each tool measured different aspects of students' learning. The performance tasks would assess students' ability to justify and find solutions, whereas quizzes would show students' facility with paper-and-pencil tasks. Investigations would allow me to observe students' perseverance, and POWs would showcase elegance in writing about their thinking. I would use one different assessment tool every four weeks. The process seemed manageable, and I hoped it would provide me with more information about my students and allow me to have more insight into their mathematical understanding and performance.

GETTING STARTED

The first month of trying my new assessment program was very informative. I saw Damon, my articulate fifth grader, shine when asked to mentally solve $300 - 10 + 21 - 3$ and verbally explain his thinking. The following week, however, I saw him cry in frustration at his inability to write down on paper similar explanations for that week's Problem of the Week. I observed Hisako, a limited-English-proficient child, happily engaged in the multiplication quiz. The following week, however, she sat apart from her peers, unwilling to participate with others in her group to investigate Fibonacci numbers appearing in nature. It was good to have different assessment tools to employ as I began to see different strengths and needs in my students.

How Do I Assess Thee?
Let Me Count the Ways …

PROBLEMS AND CONCERNS

Things did not continue as smoothly, however, as the months wore on. "Your math class is easier than it was last year. We don't have to do as much. When you did POWs every week, we were more challenged," exclaimed Louis, a gifted mathematical problem solver. "I don't like four different things a month; it's too confusing," stated Jessica, commenting on the assessment tools. "Am I improving in math? What am I doing good in and where do I need more help?" asked Rie, who has a reading learning disability. These and other questions continued to pop up, and I began to wonder myself as I plowed along, maintaining my planned assessment course.

By the first report card period, I could not tell if any student had shown progress in any one area. What did each student really know? The four assessment tools should have helped, but I found myself not able to remember how each student did on POWs, on performance tasks, on investigations, or on completing quizzes. In previous years, I prided myself on knowing that I could rely on my observations of an individual student's growth over time. I could pinpoint particular difficult concepts or skills. I could remember conversations that I held with each student. But now, I couldn't keep track of everyone in all four areas of assessment. I began to wonder, "Did a variety of information really mean more information? What did I really know about each child's mathematical knowledge or performance—just that she did well on one POW about logic, average on an investigation of patterns, and had difficulty performing mental math calculations? How many of each assessment type was enough; how many of each strand within the assessments was enough? Was Damon, the articulate fifth grader, remembering how to write POWs successfully when we worked on them only once a month? And do the different types of POWs show how much he learned in one math strand, or are there inconsistencies if I vary these as well?"

Changing methods of instruction and trying to use different types of assessment were overwhelming. I wasn't sure whether I could continue. Now I had received too much information about a lot of stuff, information about sixty students, but I did not have enough quality information about a few important concepts. It was difficult counting all those ways to know a child's mathematical understanding. In reality, was a variety of assessment tools too much for one teacher to undertake?

CHAPTER *1*

Primary Portfolios

I love teaching math in the primary grades, but it is often a challenge. Many students come to school eager to read books and learn new words, but not as many are eager to work with numbers. I teach in a multiage primary class of six-, seven-, and eight-year-olds, and I believe that all students can succeed in mathematics. I try to set high expectations for my students and am usually willing to make changes in my teaching and assessment to help my students meet these expectations.

STATE REFORM MANDATES

My teaching and assessment practices have changed dramatically over the past eight years. In mathematics, I was a very traditional teacher, using the textbook and drill-and-practice exercises often. I was comfortable and confident with the way I taught mathematics to my students. My assessment was straightforward—homework, quizzes, mad minutes for drill, and tests. Then, along came state reform mandates for primary classrooms, and our state legislature passed laws that influenced the way students were taught and assessed in primary schools. These mandates influenced my mathematics teaching more than my teaching in any other subject.

Teachers had to use hands-on materials and cooperative groups. They had to integrate subjects through thematic units. Primary classrooms had to be multiage and include at least two different age groups. The new state assessment included open-ended questions, group performance events, and math portfolios. Because of these, teachers had to create new types of classroom assessment, learn to score students' work, and give students and others effective feedback. I had to rethink completely the way that I taught and assessed my students' learning.

The pressure was on all primary school teachers in my state. The stakes of accountability were high—teachers could receive cash rewards for high student performance or they could lose their jobs for low student performance. The pressure was perhaps greatest on fourth-grade teachers at the beginning of the reform mandates. Students took the first battery of written assessments, which included satisfactory math portfolios, in that grade.

As a teacher of first through third graders, I too felt the pressure. I knew that I had to help my students build an understanding of mathematics. They needed to develop computational and problem-solving skills to do well on the fourth-grade assessment. They also needed to develop the mathematical language necessary to write about mathematics in portfolios. In addition, they needed to understand how mathematics is used in real-life settings outside schools. This learning had to begin in my primary school class.

Primary Portfolios

TRYING NEW ASSESSMENT APPROACHES

The new teaching approaches and assessments were not easy to implement; I was so comfortable with my old ways of teaching and testing. After attending some workshops and thinking long and hard about what I was being required to do, I realized that the changes might actually be valuable to my students, especially in mathematics.

I began making changes with portfolio tasks. I developed tasks connected to my mathematics curriculum. I found a few books that contained mathematics portfolio tasks, but I preferred creating my own tasks to address the needs and interests of my students. In addition, my students seemed to enjoy these tasks. The more I used math portfolio tasks in my classroom, the more I could see how they helped my students see mathematics in real-life situations. I also saw my students improve their reasoning skills through these tasks.

SOME CHALLENGES

Despite the advantages I saw in portfolios, I ran into several problems during my first year of using them. Storage was a major problem. Trying to find room for the extra folders and making them accessible to the students were my first problems in portfolio management. Getting six-, seven-, and eight-year-old students to take responsibility for their papers was not easy.

Finding good mathematics tasks that aligned with my curriculum was also a problem. Since I had relied so heavily on the textbook, I did not have good sources for other kinds of tasks. I often had to develop my own, and I had to be creative and spontaneous. Finding mathematics tasks that can be used effectively in a multiage classroom proved difficult. How could one task mathematically challenge six-year-olds and eight-year-olds equally well? The tasks must be open-ended so that many solutions are possible.

Developing rubrics was another problem for me. In my old system, answers were either right or wrong. If they weren't right, I knew how to give partial credit. Designing rubrics that captured students' thinking at a variety of levels was new. I tried to get my students involved in developing rubrics from the outset of the school year, so that we all could learn together. To illustrate how I put my changes into action, I will share a task that I developed for Saint Patrick's Day.

CHAPTER *1*

Primary Portfolios

A SAINT PATRICK'S DAY TASK

I gave students bags of Lucky Charms cereal and asked them to estimate, sort, and graph the types of cereal in their bags. I also asked them to respond to these questions: "Leprechauns are fond of clovers. Would a leprechaun like your bag of Lucky Charms? Why or why not?" The students helped me develop a rubric to assess their finished products. After some discussion, we developed the rubric that follows. (See **fig. 1.15**.)

FIG. 1.15

SAINT PATRICK'S DAY RUBRIC

4   Student answers the question "Why would the leprechaun like the bag of cereal?" Gives good explanation why. Discusses the findings in a graph. Discusses the most, the least, and so on. Makes many comparisons about the findings. Good mathematical language is used. All findings and graph match.

3   Student answers the question "Why would the leprechaun like the bag of cereal?" Gives an explanation why. Discusses the findings in a graph. Makes some comparisons about findings. Uses some mathematical language. Most of the findings and graph match.

2   Student attempts to answer "Why would the leprechaun like the bag of cereal?" Tries to give an answer. Makes a few comparisons about his or her findings. Uses a few mathematical words. A few of the findings and graph match.

1   Student attempts to answer "Why would the leprechaun like the bag of cereal?" Makes one or two comparisons on his or her graph or none at all. Many of the findings do not match the graph.

0   Student doesn't attempt an answer. Makes no comparisons.

Primary Portfolios

The students started the activity by estimating how many Lucky Charms they had. Next they sorted the different types of Lucky Charms and counted them by using tally sheets. After they sorted and counted their cereal, they displayed their results on a graph. We then discussed our findings as a class. We discussed the rubric once again so that every student clearly understood the expectations. Working in pairs, students then answered the questions, "Would a leprechaun like your bag of cereal? Why or why not? " Their work was revealing. Below is an example of one student's work. Note how the child used graphs and explained her findings. (See **figs. 1.16** and **1.17**.)

FIG. 1.16

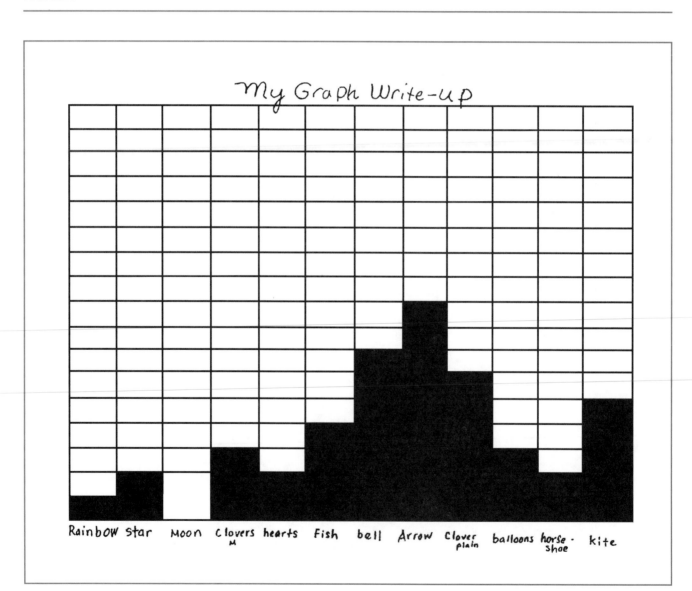

My Graph Write-up

Rainbow star Moon Clovers hearts Fish bell Arrow Clover plain balloons horse-shoe kite

FIG. 1.17

My Graph write up

I don't think the leprecnaun would like my sack of "lucky charms" because I had 1 rainbow, 2 stars, 3 marshmellow cloves, 2 hearts, 4 Fish, 7 bells, 9 arrows, 6 plain clovers, 3 ballons, 2 hores shoes, and 5 kites. The leprechan likes the marshmellow clovers the best and I only have three marshmellow cloues. I think the leprechan likes the green clover as well because it not only brings us luck but him as well. The title of my graph is "My Yummy lucky charm graph" The rainbow, the stars, the moons, One kind of the clovers, the hearts, the balloons the horse shoes and the kites are all marshmellows, Fish, the bell, the arrow, and one kind of the clovers are plain. The least I had was moon because no one picked it. The most I had was the arrow shapes second was the bell shapes and clover plain shapes were third. I had 44 luckcharms all together. After we tallied our charms and graphed them then we could eat them. That was the best part.

The task was a challenge for my six-year-olds but pretty easy for my eight-year-olds. I am still trying to think of ways to challenge my eight-year-olds with this task.

THE MORE I LEARN ...

I have seen great improvement in my students' mathematics performance in the three years I have had them. I believe that my students are ready for mathematics portfolios in the fourth grade. I love teaching mathematics more than ever, and I have a pretty clear focus of what I want to accomplish with my students. But I am no longer as comfortable with my teaching and assessment as I once was. The more I learn about my students, the more I realize how hard really good assessment is.

When the Wrong Way Works

As I walked into school on Thursday morning, I was feeling frustrated. I had just graded a mathematics quiz for my class of fifth graders. Most students had done well, but the group of Jan, Hector, Sue, and Molly had missed almost every problem involving the subtraction of fractions. They seemed to have no idea what the proper method was. They were finding the common denominator, but they seemed to have no idea what to do with the numerators. For example, each group member had solved 4/15 – 1/5 as 4/15 – 1/15 = 1/5.

I was really surprised. The day before the quiz, the group had correctly solved all three examples I had given the class as a quick diagnostic assessment. In fact, as they left the class, the group made a point of telling me that they had been having trouble but must now be "on track" since they had them all right. I knew the four students would be as disappointed and surprised as I was.

DIGGING DEEPER

I decided to interview the group the next day before giving back the quiz. Luckily, part of the class was to be devoted to teamwork on the "Problem of the Week" so I could talk to the group without singling them out.

I began math period the next day with a short introduction to the Problem of the Week. Then, I moved from group to group, checking in. When I joined Jan, Hector, Sue, and Molly, I ignored the Problem of the Week and focused on fractions immediately. I wrote down "3/10 – 1/4" on a piece of paper so all four students could see. Then I asked, "How would you explain how to do this subtraction to someone who does not know how to do it?"

The group huddled for a minute, and Molly began. "First, you find the common denominator. For this one, it's 20."

"Great," I said. "Jan, can you tell me why it is 20?"

"Sure," Jan replied. "Four doesn't go into 10, but it does go into 20, which is the next multiple of 10."

"Okay," I said. "Keep going."

"Well, the next step is to subtract the numerators. Three minus one is two so the answer is two-twentieths." Jan took the marker and wrote "3/20 – 1/20 = 2/20."

"But," Molly jumped back in, "that can be reduced to one-tenth."

I now knew that they did not understand the process and had simply memorized a method. They left out the important step of finding equivalent fractions; but I was still confused as to their thinking. I asked, "Could you show me the problem on a number line?"

When the Wrong Way Works

The students drew a number line and labeled 3/10. After a little discussion within the group, they drew a mark halfway between 2/10 and 3/10 and labeled it 1/4. Jan drew a brace to show the difference. (See **fig. 1.18**.)

I prompted, "How big is that?"

"One-half of one-tenth," said Jan.

"Which is one-twentieth," added Sue.

"But that doesn't match! It's one-tenth the other way," said Jan.

I could see the students were uncomfortable with having two answers. Hector had been quiet in the conversation so far. What was he thinking? I suggested, "Let's try a third way to see which one is right. Hector, why don't you write for us?"

"Molly, what was that common denominator?"

"Twenty."

"Hector, how many twentieths is three-tenths?"

"Six."

"One-fourth?"

"Five."

I asked Hector to write a sentence and Hector wrote "6/20 – 5/20."

All four students said, "1/20 must be right."

BUT THEY WERE RIGHT!

Then Jan rustled through his book to find a paper. "But the other method worked great on Tuesday. Look!"

Jan displayed the work from the *practice test*.

$$4/5 - 2/3 = 2/15 \qquad 3/4 - 1/2 = 1/4 \qquad 6/7 - 1/2 = 5/14$$

"Mr. Jonsen, these all checked out right. What happened?"

I did a quick check. Sure enough they were correct. By chance, I had assigned three problems with solutions that could be arrived at using the mistaken algorithm the students had "created."

NOW WHAT?

My mind was racing. Why did these examples "work" the wrong way? How could I have taught differently so that the students would not have even considered doing the computations without finding equivalent fractions? For now, though, I had to get back to the group. It was time for a mini-lesson that would show them the "right way" to subtract fractions, but I needed to be gentle to avoid crushing their confidence in figuring out things for themselves.

"Well, your answers *were* right. The examples I chose *could* be done the way you've been working. I'm sorry you got the wrong impression, but we've seen that your way doesn't work all the time. We've got to make sure you learn a way that works every time. Let's look at a couple more examples."

FIG. 1.18

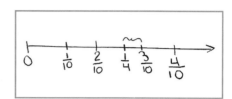

Chapter 2

Cases about Scoring Assessment

A Team Approach

At Clark School, the faculty had spent two years revamping the scope and sequence of the grades K–4 mathematics program. The new "Clark Mathematics Outcomes" document was organized using the NCTM *Standards*, and the sequence was designed around manipulative-based student learning rather than worksheets and "teacher telling." In summer work sessions, teachers designed a variety of assessments for each of the skills and concepts that students were expected to learn. Yet, they had made no systematic effort to assess and document students' problem-solving achievement. If problem solving was to be central to their program, teachers realized they needed a way to assess this complex area of student achievement.

At an afternoon meeting called to discuss this issue, teachers agreed to pilot problem-solving assessment tasks with their students. Each student in grades 1–4 would participate in a performance task each quarter. At the end of the year, teachers would decide if the scores on these tasks painted a good picture of student achievement.

DESIGNING THE TASKS

The first-grade team was now on its second task of the year. At an earlier meeting, the three teachers, Ann, Don, and Tina, had chosen the four tasks for the year from a commercially available set of tasks designed for first-grade students. For the first task, students had designed two-dimensional patterns. At the scoring meeting for this task, teachers were impressed by the level of students' responses, but they were also concerned that they might not be getting an equitable measure of students' performance. Each teacher had used slightly different materials, and these differences showed in the variety of patterns that the students produced. Ann and Tina had taken dictation for some students' explanations, whereas Don had not. Did this put Don's students at a disadvantage?

The second task, "The Party," prompted students to write number sentences about a picture. In advance, the teachers agreed on the wording to be used to introduce the task and on what materials would be available in all three classes. They also decided that all students would write their responses and then read them to their teachers who, in turn, would make notes so that "inventive spellings" would be understandable at scoring time.

DECIDING ON CRITERIA

Ann, Don, and Tina came to the scoring meeting with their students' work. They settled into seats at a corner of the large conference room table and took a minute to review the 4-point rubric and anchor papers that came with the task. The rubric classified students' work into four categories: 4 — expert, 3 — proficient, 2 — basic, and 1 — novice. In a short discussion, the three agreed that accuracy, number of examples, and organization were the important features. Since the task said "use numbers, words, or pictures," the form or quality of writing was not to be an issue in scoring.

A Team Approach

SCORING THE TASKS

Tina took the first stack. She held up the top paper and read the student's response out loud. Each teacher scored the response and compared their scores. They all matched, and a score of 3 was recorded. On the next paper, Ann and Tina thought a score of 2 described the response, whereas Don believed that it better matched the 3 level on the rubric.

Tina, who often acted as a moderator for the group, said, "Let's go back to the examples in the book." The teachers went back to the photocopies of the rubric and anchor papers.

Don pointed to a 3 example on page 27 and commented, "Except for handwriting, Scott's paper is almost identical to this one. Actually, he has a little more detail."

The others agreed, commenting that the immature writing may have influenced their scoring. Tina added, "I need to remember that "neatly written" is something we are *working on* but not scoring right now."

The scoring continued with Ann, Tina, and Don in consensus until the group got to Mark's paper. Mark had written several numerals and made a few drawings on his paper. The numbers and drawings did not match the picture. Don and Tina scored the paper a 1, and Ann, his teacher, gave it a score of 3.

Ann spoke immediately, "But this is Mark. This is good work for him. At the beginning of the year, he couldn't even make numerals and wouldn't sit still long enough to finish anything. He's come such a long way. He deserves more than a 1."

Don responded gently, "We're not scoring Mark; we're just scoring his paper. It's important to keep that in mind as we work."

Tina added, "I know where you are coming from, but if we end up using these scores in student profiles, it is important that the numbers mean something. A 3 can't mean one thing for student A and something else for student B. Teachers after us need to know what students can do, not how hard they are trying."

Ann responded, "It's the record I'm worried about. It's not fair to label Mark as a 1 student. His parents will see this, and I don't want them to think that with all his work and their work, he hasn't progressed. The 1 just doesn't tell Mark's story."

The second session ended with teachers wondering how to resolve the issue they had encountered. They wondered if other groups of teachers had similar problems in scoring students' work.

If They Only Knew Michael

In the course of working with a professional development group focused on authentic assessment in mathematics, my colleagues and I decided we would each give the following task in our classrooms and score it together the next time we met. I administered the task to my fourth graders late in the school year. (See **fig. 2.1**.)

FIG. 2.1

You have been saving money for a weekend party. You opened your piggy bank and found that you have $7.98. You want to invite four of your best friends to the party. Your mother will take you to the store to buy snacks for the group, and among the snacks, you must choose at least two healthy items. You must to decide what to buy from the following:

six-pack of soda	$1.69
large bag of potato chips	$1.89
half-gallon of ice cream	$3.69
four frozen minipizzas	$3.59
bag of six oranges	$1.94
candy bar	$0.75
microwave popcorn (3-pack box)	$3.69
half-gallon of milk	$1.56
pint of frozen yogurt	$1.80
cookies	$2.09

(a) List the items you would like to buy at the store and show their total cost. Be sure that—

■ the money you have left over from your $7.98 is not enough to buy anything else;

■ you have chosen at least two healthy items.

(b) Explain how and why you selected each item on your list.

CHAPTER *2*

If They Only Knew Michael

I had often asked the children to write explanations of their thinking in mathematics. I explained that this time they were helping a group of teachers who were trying to develop better ways to assess what children know. These teachers would be the only ones who would see their papers. The students accepted their role very earnestly and worked hard on the assessment.

My colleagues and I had modified the initial task to clarify what was being asked. For example, we specified the quantities of some items to clarify amounts. We changed "four frozen pizzas" to "four frozen minipizzas." We inserted "3-pack box" to describe the microwave popcorn. We thought our modifications would encourage the students to write a clear rationale for their selection. We hoped students would provide an explanation of how the amount of each item might be distributed among their friends, such as stating, "There are four minipizzas, so we will share them so that five people can eat them."

GIVING THE TASK

I took about half an hour to present the task and answer my students' many questions. Many of these questions were about quantities. One student asked, "How many cookies do you get for $2.09?"

I answered, "Let's say it's an average-sized package, like Oreos."

"Is the candy bar jumbo size?" asked another.

"No, it's an individual, regular-sized candy bar," I said. I brought in one-half gallon and pint containers to be sure that the children understood these amounts.

"Is there tax on the food?"

"No, there is no tax on this food," I assured the class.

I thought I had made it clear that I wanted to be able to understand their thinking from what I would read on their papers. I hoped they would write out the process they used and their strategy for how they arrived at their food choices as well. I was looking for explanations like "I started by choosing cookies because I like them, but when I added up all my food I found I still had $2.03 left, so then I put in the bag of oranges to use up the rest of the money"; or "I bought too much, and then I had to go back and take it out and choose the candy bar instead because it was less money." To my disappointment, many students answered the "explain how you selected each item" part of the task by making statements like "I chose ice cream because my friends like it." Few students actually explained a numerical strategy.

If They Only Knew Michael

SCORING THE TASK

I took all the students' work to our next assessment meeting. The scoring procedure that our assessment group followed was to divide the papers initially into two piles: "Ready for Revision" (RR) and "More Instruction Needed" (MI). Later, we subdivided each pile into two according to a 4-point rubric. We agreed on the following criteria: for a paper to be considered RR, it must have correct mathematics, including showing the funds insufficient to buy more items. It must also have some sort of rationale for the choices of items. Anything less would consign a paper to the MI pile.

We discussed what the rationale should look like. Although we really wanted to see explanations about how they arrived at their choices, we knew that very few students had written these. We decided that if the student gave any rationale at all, such as "I chose oranges because they are healthy" or "I chose potato chips because everyone likes them," his or her paper would meet the criteria.

I, and perhaps all of us, had agreed to criteria for RR and MI without really discussing in depth what we considered the most important aspects of this task. We evidently were not explicit enough about what "showing that funds were insufficient to buy more items" meant. Once we started scoring, we found ourselves disagreeing.

One person argued, "Showing means we have to see it written out that just seventeen cents is left."

Another countered, "That's ridiculous! If a student shows that $7.83 was spent, it's obvious that not enough remains for another purchase." I wondered to myself if the students wouldn't agree with this statement.

CHAPTER 2

If They Only Knew Michael

MICHAEL'S PAPER

Michael, an intelligent, articulate boy in my class who has no trouble with written expression, turned in the paper shown in **figure** 2.2.

FIG. 2.2

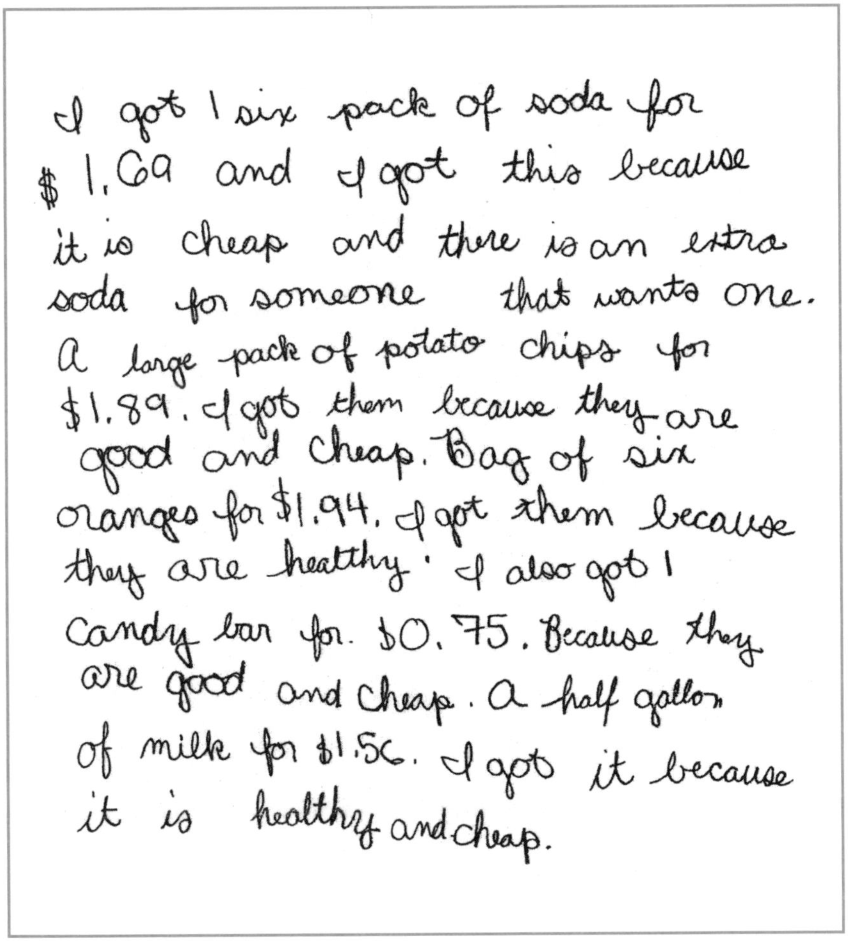

I got 1 six pack of soda for $1.69 and I got this because it is cheap and there is an extra soda for someone that wants one. A large pack of potato chips for $1.89. I got them because they are good and cheap. Bag of six oranges for $1.94. I got them because they are healthy. I also got 1 candy bar for $0.75. Because they are good and cheap. A half gallon of milk for $1.56. I got it because it is healthy and cheap.

If They Only Knew Michael

When we began scoring Michael's paper, I was the only one that had placed it in the RR group. I had based my evaluation both on the knowledge that I had about my student and on my checking of his mathematics. I inferred he knew the total cost and that he didn't have enough money left over to buy something else, even though he didn't explicitly state it. But, as we discussed our disagreement, I had to concur that Michael's work indeed did not qualify as RR according to our criteria.

I was left troubled by my inability to stick to the scoring criteria as well as by the discrepancy between what Michael produced and my knowledge of him. Ironically, I think he would have made a better showing on a traditional test than he had on this "authentic" assessment question. I wondered: "How can I be 'objective' scoring my own students' work?" And, thinking back to why I wasn't getting the explanations I wanted, "How could I help my students produce the quality of work I think they are capable of doing? How can I get them to write their entire thinking process?"

CHAPTER *2*

Students as Assessors

There are many players in the assessment process. Depending on the purpose of assessment, the players can include teachers, parents, students, and administrators. As a fourth-grade teacher, I was concerned that my students did not see themselves as part of that process. Rather, they viewed themselves as passive recipients of grades; assessment was something that happened to them.

THE PROBLEM

To give my students a chance to play a more active role in the assessment process, I wanted to create a situation where my students became the assessors. In March, I gave my class of eighteen students a problem to solve. The problem, from the book *The Power of Two*, read as follows:

> Mickey Mouse was the sorcerer's apprentice in the movie Fantasia. *He plays with magic to get a broom to carry water for him. When the broom gets out of control, Mickey hits it with a hatchet and it splits into two brooms. Then those two brooms split into four brooms, and Mickey is in big powers-of-2 trouble! If you begin with one broom and the doubling occurs every 15 seconds, how many brooms will be carrying water at the end of 5 minutes?*

I told students to work in their prearranged groups in order to find a solution to the problem. They had to work together to come up with a presentation that showed how they solved the problem. Since this was the first time they had to solve a problem and communicate their solution to other students, I did not want to overwhelm them by requiring them to write out their thinking process. They could talk about what they did as part of the presentation. Everyone in each group had to understand the solution and be able to explain it. Although they would be scored on their presentations, I did not offer scoring criteria. The students did not ask for any.

Students as Assessors

GROUP SOLUTIONS

The five group presentations included four different answers and three distinct solution strategies. Three of the groups arrived at incorrect answers, but each group had a strategy that could lead to the right solution. Josh's group presented its solution on a poster. It had an incorrect answer and appeared as follows:

5×60 seconds $= 300$ seconds   300 seconds $\div 15 = 20$ times it will split

1 broom

$2^1 = 2$ brooms	$2^{11} = 2\,048$ brooms
$2^2 = 4$ brooms	$2^{12} = 4\,096$ brooms
$2^3 = 8$ brooms	$2^{13} = 8\,192$ brooms
$2^4 = 16$ brooms	$2^{14} = 16\,384$ brooms
$2^5 = 32$ brooms	$2^{15} = 32\,786$ brooms
$2^6 = 64$ brooms	$2^{16} = 65\,572$ brooms
$2^7 = 128$ brooms	$2^{17} = 131\,144$ brooms
$2^8 = 256$ brooms	$2^{18} = 262\,288$ brooms
$2^9 = 512$ brooms	$2^{19} = 524\,576$ brooms
$2^{10} = 1\,024$ brooms	$2^{20} = 1\,049\,152$ brooms

When the presentations were over, I asked, "Which of these is the correct answer and how do you know?" Together the students arrived at the correct answer by comparing the posters and finding the computation errors in three of the presented solutions. (At no time during the presentations did I comment about the answers.)

Students as Assessors

SCORING PRIORITIES

I then posed the question, "Now that you're finished with the presentations, I need to give each group a score. How do you think I should do that? Only two groups had the correct answer, but in your discussion you found that each group had a solution strategy that could have worked if the group had not made a computation error. What should I do?"

After a few awkward moments the students started to offer suggestions.

Tommy:	Well, everyone who got the right answer should get an A.
Kristin:	No, everybody who had a good strategy should get an A. That's more important than the right answer.
Teacher:	Well, that is an interesting point. Is a correct strategy more important than a right answer in math?
Paul:	You need both!
Kristin:	But Josh's group didn't get the right answer and they had a good solution strategy. They just multiplied wrong once.
Teacher:	This is an interesting discussion. Teachers talk about this a lot when they have to give a score. What is important in solving problems? Is the correct answer the most important thing when you do math? What do you think?
Ken:	Sure it is. If you get the wrong answer, the teacher always marks it wrong.
Kristin:	Yeah, but sometimes if you do everything right and just make one little mistake, you only get 1 point off. I think it is more important that you know how to do it, even if you just make one little adding mistake.
Teacher:	What other things do you think are important when you solve a problem?
Suzy:	It is important that everybody works together in a group.
Teacher:	That's a good point, Suzy. Does anyone have any other suggestions?
Louis:	It is important that the group explains themselves good so everyone knows what they did.
Teacher:	That is another good point, Louis. We've had a lot of good suggestions here. Right now I'm going to give you time in your groups. Your group's job is to come up with four criteria that you think I should consider when I give your group a score for the presentation. We've just talked about a few of them. You can use them if you think they are important or come up with others.

Students as Assessors

At this point, the students went back into groups to generate a list of criteria for assessing their presentations. I hoped that our class discussion would encourage them to come up with criteria that was more complex than just "getting the right answer," such as valuing a good solution strategy or being able to talk out their mathematical thinking.

The next day the small groups shared their list of criteria with the large group. I wrote each group's original suggestions on the board, and together we combined similar criteria and deleted others until everyone agreed with the list. For example, one group suggested "a good explanation" as one criterion. Another group said, "Everybody has to understand how the group got its answer." Another group said, "We think it is important that the group tells what strategy they used." To my disappointment, no one suggested "has a strategy that could lead to a correct answer." By combining their suggestions, we came up with "Group explains its solution strategy step by step."

Since my fourth graders had no experience with rubrics but were used to numeric scores based on a 100-point scale, I decided to have them work on a scoring scale. I wanted the students to assign points to each criterion and justify their decision on how they distributed the points. There were to be a total of 100 points. To this end, I asked them to think about "Are all these criterion equally important or are some more important than others?" Each child received a copy of the agreed-on criteria in order to consider the answer to this question for homework. (See **fig. 2.3**.)

FIG. 2.3

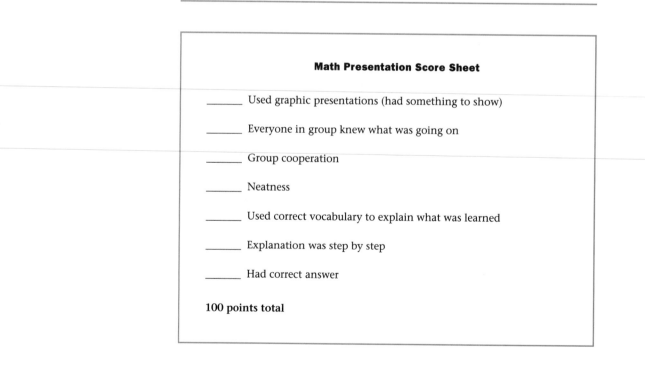

Math Presentation Score Sheet

_____ Used graphic presentations (had something to show)

_____ Everyone in group knew what was going on

_____ Group cooperation

_____ Neatness

_____ Used correct vocabulary to explain what was learned

_____ Explanation was step by step

_____ Had correct answer

100 points total

CHAPTER 2

Students as Assessors

The next day, student discussion turned toward reaching agreement on the points that each criterion would be worth. After each student offered his or her points for *using graphic representations* (which meant using pictures, drawings, or visual aids) and one boy recorded these on the board, I asked, "How do we decide how many points to assign to 'graphic representations' so that everyone's opinions are considered?" Several students suggested averaging the points. They did this and came up with an average of 7. However, several students thought this was not representative, since no individual in the class actually assigned 7 points to this criterion. The class ultimately decided to use the most frequently occurring score, 15.

It was very interesting to me how the number of points that a student assigned to each criterion revealed his or her values in mathematics. The criterion that generated the greatest amount of discussion was "had correct answer." It was very clear to me that one boy who assigned 40 points to this criterion thought mathematics was about right answers and not about coming up with good solution strategies. Since many students agreed with him, I found myself wondering how I could instill in all my students an appreciation for a good solution strategy and the process someone goes through to solve a problem. As I looked at our final list, I wondered what I could do in the future to have them develop the values I wanted them to have in mathematics class.

During the remainder of the school year, I wanted the students to assess one another's presentations using their scoring scale, but there were not many opportunities to do this. I wondered what would have happened if I had started the process early in the school year. Would this have helped them come up with deeper and more-complex criteria? Would having them go through this process of self-assessment from the beginning of the year help them become better problem solvers?

Chapter 3

Cases about Using Assessment Results

The New Student

In January, Ashley came to my multiage first- and second-grade classroom from a regular first-grade classroom in a small community nearby. When she arrived, my class had already completed numeration to 19 and had spent at least two months on numeration to 99. Our study of numbers included hands-on activities, done both in large and small groups, that used base-ten blocks, Unifix cubes, and collections of sortable objects. According to Ashley's transfer report, she had experienced only numbers up to five and had worked primarily from a workbook. Because my class is multiage, my first graders have been exposed to much of the second-grade curriculum. My first thoughts were "How will I ever catch her up?" and "Will she be able to adjust to a different approach to math?"

Shortly after she arrived, I gave my first graders a posttest on numeration. This was the first time they had taken a formal mathematics test. I decided to give it to Ashley as well, even though I knew it was beyond what she had done in her previous school. I hoped it would give me insight into where to begin. Ashley didn't attempt anything on the test. Even though I spent some time with her during the test, it was evident to me that she had no understanding of place value. She could not recognize the words *tens* or *ones*. She was totally bewildered. (See **fig. 3.1**.)

FIG. 3.1

Written Assessment Task NOS -I

Name: Date: Score:

OBJECTIVE: Identifies and names place value, reads and writes whole numbers (0–100).

1. In 65 there are _____ tens.

2. In 90 there are _____ ones.

3. In 85 there are _____ ones.

4. In 8 there are _____ tens.

For questions 5 to 8, write the correct number.

5. 8 ones and 2 tens = _____

6. 4 tens and 0 ones = _____

7. 6 ones and 7 tens = _____

8. 0 tens and 5 ones = _____

The New Student

From the blank test results, I knew I needed to assess Ashley individually in order to find out what she knew and if she could demonstrate her understanding of numbers. I decided to interview her in the afternoon, when the classroom assistant was present. Then I could spend a few minutes alone with Ashley. First, I asked her to write numbers as high as she could. She did so hesitantly and struggled to write the numbers, particularly after ten. (See **fig. 3.2**.)

FIG. 3.2

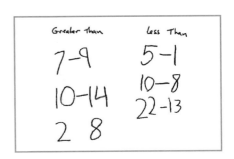

1 2 3 4 5 6 7 8 9 10 11 12 13 14 15
17 18 19 20 21 22 23 24 25

FIG. 3.3

Then, I had her write numbers that were less than or greater than another number. For example, I said "7" and asked her to write a number that was greater than 7. She did fine until I gave her the number 28. Her work showed that she understood *less than* and *greater than*, but she got stuck with the larger number (28). (See **fig. 3.3**.)

Greater than	Less Than
7–9	5–1
10–14	10–8
2 8	22–13

Next, I asked Ashley to write numbers in a sequence. (See **fig. 3.4**.) She did okay as long as the numbers increased by one. She had difficulty, however, writing numbers that skipped (e.g., 2, 4, 6, ...).

Her understanding of one-to-one correspondence was good. I gave her nine counters and asked her to count out the same number. She counted them by making a matching set and lining her objects up directly underneath mine. Then I put out two sets of six counters. One set was spread out and the other set was close together. I asked her which set had more. Her response was, "The top has more. The bottom is shorter." When she saw me writing, she counted them and announced, "I think they're both the same. They have six."

FIG. 3.4

5, 6, 7, 8, 9, 10
10, 11, 12, 13, 14, 15
2, 4, 6, 7, 8, 9
3, 5, 7, 8, 9, 10
10, 9, 8, 7, 6, 5

The New Student

FIG. 3.5

1 4 0000000000
0000

I then had Ashley empty a container of counters onto the table. When I asked her to count them for me, she counted them correctly one by one up to fourteen. Then I asked her to make a group of ten. She did so with the counters and then drew a picture of what she had done. (See **fig. 3.5**.)

I asked her about the digits 1 and 4 in the number 14, but she couldn't make connections to what she had just done. I explained it to her.

I asked her to do the same with the number 22. She made two groups of ten counters and two single counters. When questioned about the meaning of the digits in the number, however, she still could not make a connection. We continued to do this with other numbers. She made 35 by counting out three groups of ten counters, with five left over. She drew the picture that way. (See **fig. 3.6**.) With guided questions, she could explain what the 3 and the 5 meant, but without prompting, she could not do so on her own.

FIG. 3.6

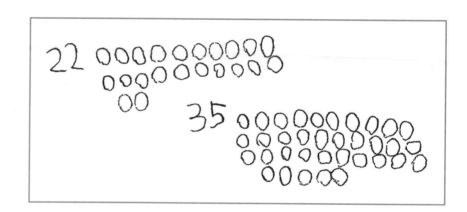

I thought at this point she was beginning to grasp the idea of place value, even though I was covering a lot of material very fast in a short time. I noticed that with each repetition of the process of making groups of ten, she became more comfortable with it. My other students had been given many opportunities to do activities like this in the time we had spent on numeration earlier in the school year.

FIG. 3.7

12 0 00

Next, I wrote the number 12 and asked Ashley to show me what she thought the number meant. She counted out twelve counters and proceeded to make a group of ten and two left over. When asked to draw it, she made the drawing shown in **figure 3.7**. She explained that the circle on the left was a group of ten. The two circles were the two left over.

The time I had alone with Ashley was up. I needed to make some decisions about what to do next. Ashley clearly needed to spend more time on place value. However, my other students were ready to move on to addition. Would Ashley be able to do addition activities? I hated to have her work by herself, but I was concerned that she would be confused if she worked with the others. It's difficult to know what's best for Ashley and still manageable to do in the classroom with twenty-one other students. How can she learn so quickly what my other students have been working on for five months?

CHAPTER 3

Melanie's Place-Value Understanding

Melanie is a second-grade student in my first- and second-grade class. After five months of school, her mathematical understanding remains a puzzle to me because of inconsistencies in her work.

When we reviewed numbers to 99 at the beginning of the year, she correctly made specific numbers using a variety of manipulatives such as base-ten blocks, Unifix cubes, and beads and posts. She also used visuals such as tens and ones stamps. She correctly wrote what I had dictated to her and read number words. She could also say what numbers came before, after, and between, and she could complete extended number patterns such as 33, 43, 53 ... On the basis of this information, I believed she was ready to progress to three-digit numbers. Since she began instruction on number concepts, however, her daily work and assessments have not given me a clear picture of her understanding.

ORDER OF THE PLACES

Watching her do seatwork, I noticed Melanie completed only a few questions each day. She answered some questions correctly but reversed the order of the places with others. For example, when using the base-ten block stamps, she stamped the ones on the left side, the tens in the middle, and the hundreds on the right side of the paper. On several questions, such as the one that follows, she seemed to ignore the place value and wrote the places in random order. She did not even write them in the order in which they were presented in the problem.

For example, she was given the chart below. After gluing the chart into her scribbler, she was to stamp the correct number of hundreds, tens, and ones and then write the numeral in standard form. On the question below, Melanie stamped the correct number of hundreds, tens, and ones but wrote "590." (See **fig. 3.8**.)

FIG. 3.8

10s	100s	1s
0	5	9

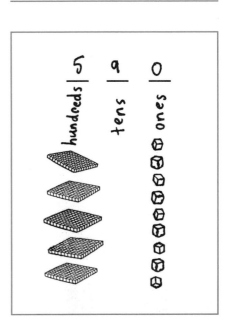

After noticing that she had not considered the order of the places, I talked to her. She explained that ones are the smallest, it takes 10 ones to make a ten; hundreds are larger than tens, and 10 tens make a hundred. As I drew an arrow from right to left, I asked her what happened to the numbers. She knew they got larger. She said they got smaller when I drew the arrow to the right. I put a reminder in her scribbler for her to refer to. Together we corrected the errors she had made. It seemed that she now knew the order of the places.

Melanie's Place-Value Understanding

Next, I had her do a similar activity, but one that required copying the number of hundreds, tens, and ones from a card. I thought that copying the information might reinforce the three places and the value of each. She did fine copying the information, but as before, she did not always consider the order of the places when stamping or writing the numeral. For example, she correctly copied the information on the following card. (See **fig. 3.9.**)

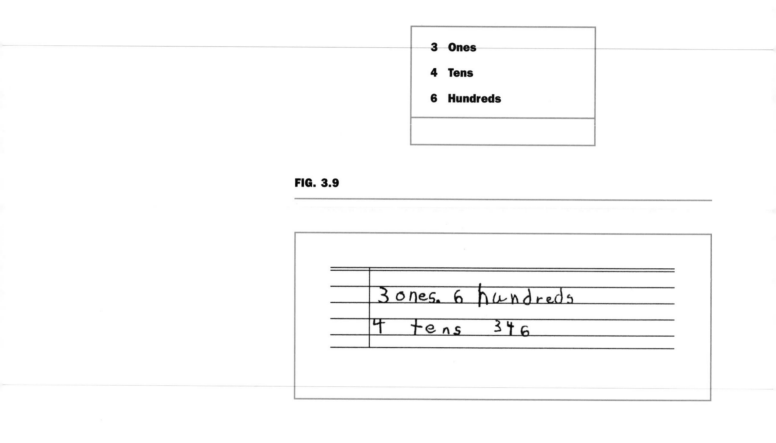

3	Ones
4	Tens
6	Hundreds

FIG. 3.9

CHAPTER *3*

Melanie's Place-Value Understanding

But when she stamped the number, this is what she did. (See **fig. 3.10**.)

FIG. 3.10

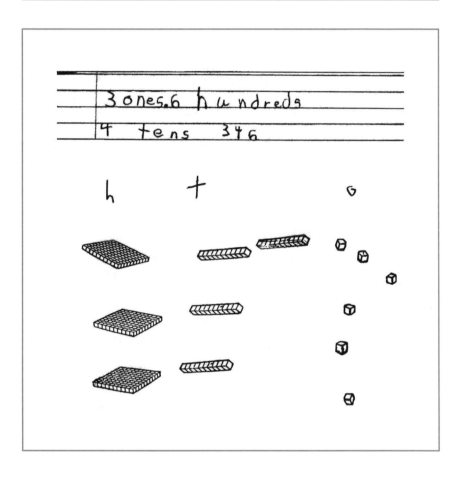

EXTENDING PATTERNS

When we were working on numeration to 999, all of my students worked on number patterns. Using base-ten blocks, they built the first number first and changed it to make the second number. Then they changed it again to make the third number, figuring out how the number was changing (i.e., which place and by how much). Finally they did the same to extend the pattern by three more numbers (e.g., 347, 357, 367, ____, ____, ____). Melanie could make the numbers but needed assistance telling how the pattern was changing so that she could extend it.

Melanie's Place-Value Understanding

WRITING DICTATED NUMBERS

The errors she made on the posttest seemed to indicate that she did not have a solid understanding of place value. For example, Melanie correctly wrote some dictated numbers, but she made errors, such as writing 404 for 440, on others. She also drew pictures to represent 6 tens, 5 ones, and 3 hundreds, but she wrote 653 instead of 365.

I decided that Melanie would benefit from continuing her work on numbers up to 999 using math trays. Although her daily work was done more accurately and with less assistance, she completed only a few questions each day. I thought her understanding had improved until I looked at her posttest. She continued to make consistent errors. When writing dictated numbers, she wrote 2 007 for 207 and 10 010 for 110. These errors were different than those she had made before. She had always written three digits. Did she really not understand that numbers in the hundreds always have three digits? She mixed up the order of the digits in some other questions, such as writing 12 for 21 and 360 for 306.

ADDING ONE-DIGIT NUMBERS

Melanie had now spent seven weeks working on three-digit numbers. The inconsistencies in her work were puzzling. Was it lack of focus or lack of understanding? Time demanded that she move on to operations. She started with work on addition questions with sums up to 18. I gave students manipulatives to help them figure out the answers. Melanie did not want to use them. She answered questions quickly. They were consistently done like those below.

$$5 + 4 = 54 \qquad 4 + 7 = 47 \qquad 3 + 8 = 38$$

I thought her errors indicated that she was confusing what we had done in place value with the process of addition. I insisted that she use concrete objects to reinforce the process of addition. With one-on-one assistance at school and help from her parents at home, Melanie did better.

REGROUPING

Melanie did well using the math trays to add and subtract with no regrouping. It seemed that her mathematical understanding was stronger and she was ready to move on to regrouping activities. In one of these activities, students were given cards like the one below.

> 3 tens 14 ones

Melanie's Place-Value Understanding

I asked the students to show me how to rewrite the number by using base-ten blocks. If necessary, they traded 10 ones for 1 ten. They then wrote the new number of tens and ones and the numeral it made. Melanie did the first one correctly when I was watching her, but she then did the following when I was not watching. (See **fig. 3.11**.) She made a new ten but kept the same number of ones. She did not write the numeral.

FIG. 3.11

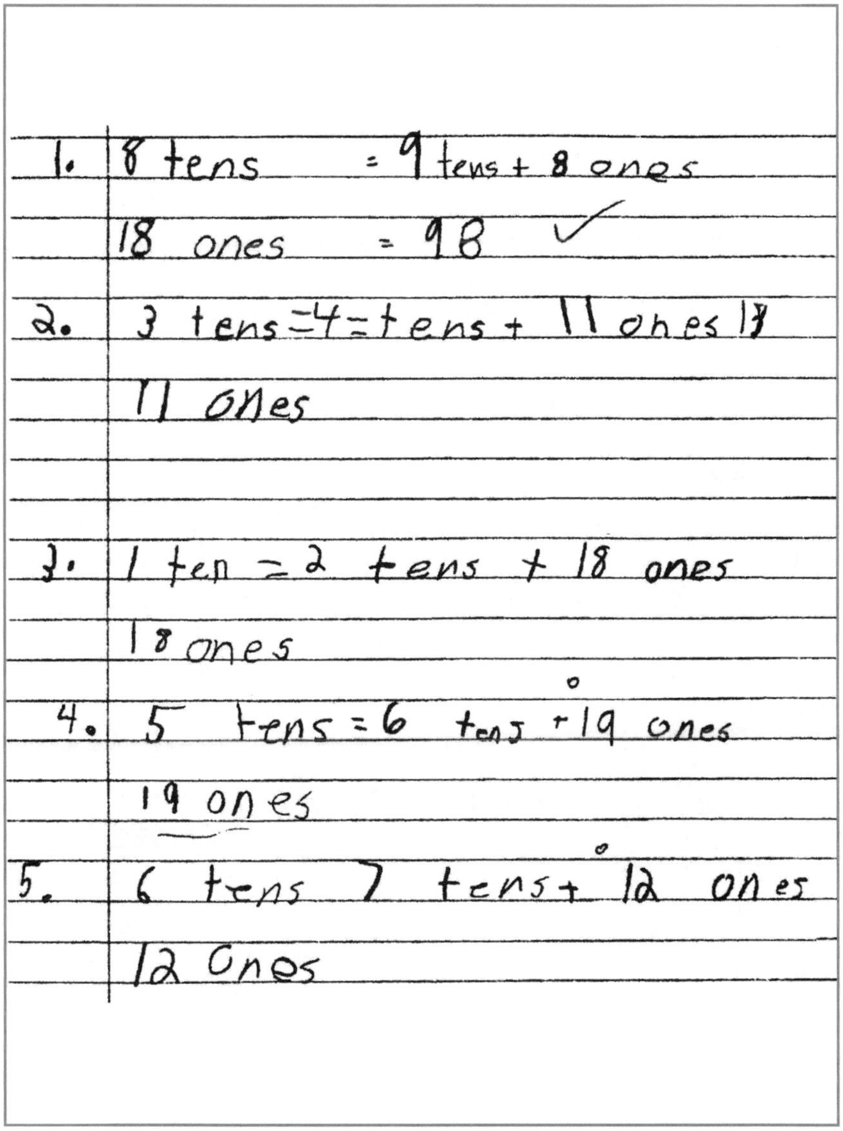

---

1. 8 tens = 9 tens + 8 ones
   18 ones = 98 ✓

2. 3 tens = 4 tens + 11 ones 17
   11 ones

3. 1 ten = 2 tens + 18 ones
   18 ones

4. 5 tens = 6 tens + 19 ones
   19 ones

5. 6 tens 7 tens + 12 ones
   12 ones

Melanie's Place-Value Understanding

With help over time, she seemed to gain a better understanding of the process. She raced through the questions on the posttest and made many errors. On the samples below, I asked her to circle 10 ones if possible, add the new ten, and write the new number of tens and ones. When I first looked at her paper, she had not circled any groups of 10 ones but had the correct number of ones written in the box. She wrote the number of tens that were there originally. I talked to her about what she had done. She corrected it by circling ten ones and making the number of tens she had written one higher. She did not draw any new tens. (See **fig. 3.12**.)

FIG. 3.12

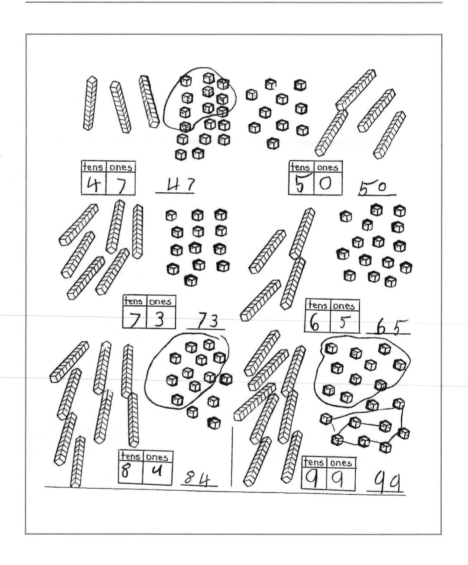

As I observed Melanie's work closely, I wondered what kinds of experiences she needs to strengthen her place-value understanding. What would help her?

CHAPTER *3*

A Rubric Solves My Problem

"Suzie feels bored in math. She also wants to make sure that she is learning the math skills for middle school next year. Isn't that what you have been telling me, Suzie?" asked Suzie's mother as we all sat down in the library for our conference.

"Yes," said Suzie, a fifth grader, in a quiet voice.

"Well, I know that she seems unhappy sometimes in math class," I replied. I thought about how glad I was that I had worked so hard to prepare for this conference. It was now early November. The mother and I had one conference at the beginning of the year, but I had been expecting a request for another because of Suzie's recent attitude in class.

"I may do a few things differently than Mr. Jones did last year," I began. "I know that is often confusing to students and their parents. Suzie is a smart girl. I am pleased that she has a firm grasp of her math facts. But, we spend a lot of time applying those facts and sharing solutions to problems that we work together."

"Before talking more about Suzie, I'd like to begin by sharing what I expect from students in my math class. Then we'll see where Suzie is in relationship to those expectations. I have tried to put my expectations in a simple form. You are the first parent to see them, so I hope you will be able to give me some feedback."

MY RUBRIC

I explained to Suzie's mother that I use a rubric to determine how well my students perform in solving problems. I showed Suzie's mother a blank copy of the rubric and explained each of the six different parts. (See **fig. 3.13** on the next page.) I discussed how I used the information gathered in class to assess each student. "I sit down with students' work, math journals, notes from observations of group work, and student interviews. I record all of this on the rubric."

A Rubric Solves My Problem

FIG. 3.13

PROBLEM SOLVING   Name _____

Understands Problem

☐ Novice   ■ Problem? What Problem?
☐ In Progress   ■ Someone else points out there is a problem
☐ Meets Expectations ■ Recognizes there is a problem independently
☐ Exceeds Expectations ■ Identifies "real" problem independently

Gathers Facts

☐ Novice   ■ Does not realize the need to find out facts. Uses any set of numbers to calculate
☐ In Progress   ■ Able to gather one or two facts independently
☐ Meets Expectations ■ Knows where to "look" to obtain additional facts
☐ Exceeds Expectations ■ Accesses information to obtain all necessary facts

Brainstorms Solutions

☐ Novice   ■ Does not generate any solutions—Does nothing or asks "What do I do?"
☐ In Progress   ■ Generates few ideas with assistance
☐ Meets Expectations ■ Generates several solutions independently
☐ Exceeds Expectations ■ Generates many creative solutions independently

Evaluates

☐ Novice   ■ Does not evaluate the effectiveness of proposed solutions
☐ In Progress   ■ Recognizes pluses and minuses of some of the solutions with assistance
☐ Meets Expectations ■ Takes time to analyze effectiveness of each possible solution independently
☐ Exceeds Expectations ■ Uses reflection to decide what to do differently next time! Recognizes a pattern or formula

Persistence

☐ Novice   ■ Gives up easily
☐ In Progress   ■ Will try with assistance
☐ Meets Expectations ■ Persists in class independently
☐ Exceeds Expectations ■ Will continue outside of classroom or come back to problem at later time

Communication

☐ Novice   ■ Cannot discuss ☐   Can show using manipulatives ☐
☐ In Progress   ■ Answers questions when asked
☐ Meets Expectations ■ Will talk with assistance about problem using appropriate mathematical language
☐ Exceeds Expectations ■ Is able to discuss using mathematical language independently

---

SUZIE'S PERFORMANCE

Turning to Suzie, I said, "I have found that although Suzie knows her math facts very well and computes well, she has some difficulties with problem solving." Bringing out a rubric that I completed on Suzie, I showed Suzie's mother how Suzie had done since the beginning of the year. (See **fig. 3.14**.)

CHAPTER *3*

A Rubric Solves My Problem

PROBLEM SOLVING

Name ___Suzie Nov. 96___

Understands Problem

☐ Novice
☑ In Progress
☐ Meets Expectations
☐ Exceeds Expectations

■ Problem? What Problem?
■ Someone else points out there is a problem
■ Recognizes there is a problem independently
■ Identifies "real" problem independently

Gathers Facts

☑ Novice
☐ In Progress
☐ Meets Expectations
☐ Exceeds Expectations

■ Does not realize the need to find out facts. Uses any set of numbers to calculate
■ Able to gather one or two facts independently
■ Knows where to "look" to obtain additional facts
■ Accesses information to obtain all necessary facts

Brainstorms Solutions

☐ Novice
☑ In Progress
☐ Meets Expectations
☐ Exceeds Expectations

■ Does not generate any solutions—Does nothing or asks "What do I do?"
■ Generates few ideas with assistance
■ Generates several solutions independently
■ Generates many creative solutions independently

Evaluates

☑ Novice
☐ In Progress
☐ Meets Expectations
☐ Exceeds Expectations

■ Does not evaluate the effectiveness of proposed solutions
■ Recognizes pluses and minuses of some of the solutions with assistance
■ Takes time to analyze effectiveness of each possible solution independently
■ Uses reflection to decide what to do differently next time! Recognizes a pattern or formula

Persistence

☐ Novice
☑ In Progress
☐ Meets Expectations
☐ Exceeds Expectations

■ Gives up easily
■ Will try with assistance
■ Persists in class independently
■ Will continue outside of classroom or come back to problem at later time

Communication

☑ Novice
☐ In Progress
☐ Meets Expectations
☐ Exceeds Expectations

■ Cannot discuss ☐   Can show using manipulatives ☐
■ Answers questions when asked
■ Will talk with assistance about problem using appropriate mathematical language
■ Is able to discuss using mathematical language independently

---

"As you can see from the first category, she is most comfortable when someone else points out problems for her. I would like to see her begin to identify problems on her own. When gathering facts, the second category, she often uses all the numbers in a word problem to do some kind of computation without a particular reason for doing so. For example, she may add numbers when she should have multiplied them. She also tends to look at problems in only one way and does not see a need for understanding another way to look at the problem."

"What exactly do you mean by that?" Suzie's mother asked.

A Rubric Solves My Problem

"Well, I want students to understand that there are sometimes many different ways to solve problems. I want them to compare the similarities and differences in strategies and to be able to determine if some strategies are better than others. Sometimes students have the idea that math is just memorizing facts and rules. They don't realize the importance of using math to solve problems or to look for patterns to help make sense of what they are doing."

"We never did that when I was in elementary school." Suzie's mother responded.

"Me either, but that's the way we often use math outside school," I replied. "Suzie is also not evaluating how reasonable her answers are. In fact, the whole class needs to work on this. I would like to see more confidence in sharing explanations of her work, too."

"Suzie never has trouble talking, does she?" asked her mother.

"Oh, no. She has no trouble talking about most things, but I have observed that she is often unsure about the mathematical language she needs to use. When students discuss their strategies with the class, talking about the problem often leads them to reflect about what they have done. Sometimes they stop in midsentence and say, 'Wait, I didn't mean to put that number! That's not right! I need to fix this!' By talking about their work, they begin to evaluate their own work."

As we ended the discussion, Suzie's mother looked at Suzie and asked, "Is your teacher right?" Sheepishly, Susie nodded yes. Suzie's mother turned to me and said, "How is she doing compared to other students in class?"

Smiling, I responded, "That's a good question, and I am working on that. I have completed rubrics on each child. Now I want to compile my class results into a chart. I will share that with you at the next conference." I explained what she could do to help Suzie at home, and Suzie and her mother left.

A Rubric Solves My Problem

DEVELOPING MY RUBRIC

I was relieved things had gone well. My rubric helped me communicate what problem-solving skills I wanted my students to develop. I had struggled for years with identifying important skills in problem solving. Coming up with an organized way to record student progress had been a challenge. Then, I took a graduate class at a local university that focused on alternative types of assessment. The class required me to read research on assessment and to develop a way to evaluate my students' mathematical skills. During class, one of my classmates shared a problem-solving rubric from IRI/Skylight Publishing. It met most of my needs. I used it immediately in my multiage classroom for third, fourth, and fifth graders. I wanted to be able to share my mathematics goals and expectations for growth and progress in a way that made sense with my students and their parents. I also wanted to describe how my students compared to each other with regard to their problem-solving skills. I wondered if these problem-solving skills were developmental or based on experience.

Initially, the rubric worked very well for me, but something was missing. I needed a more detailed way to keep track of each student. So I created a checklist. I also thought of Tony and Kathy, who often continued to work outside of class and came back the next day to share, with much excitement, the patterns they had found. One was a third grader and the other was a fifth grader, and both were accomplishing more than I had expected. So, I added "communication skills" and "persistence in problem solving." Both were important components of problem solving to me.

I shared my new rubric with a colleague. We talked about the need to be *user friendly* and about how we might record information over a three-year period. As a result of our discussion, I made another change and added "communication using manipulatives." We both agreed that was important.

A Rubric Solves My Problem

STUDENT COMPARISONS

Yes, my new rubric had helped me prepare for the conference with Suzie and her mother. I am looking forward to my next parent conference now. But, the question that Suzie's mother asked at the end of the conference suddenly renewed my interest in compiling class results. A chart may tell me even more and allow me to tell other parents where their children stand in my class.

I sat down with my individual rubrics and compiled a class chart. (See **fig. 3.15**.)

FIG. 3.15

Identifies Problem	3rd	4th	5th	Total Students
Novice	1	0	0	1
In Progress	4	5	5	14
Meets Expectations	2	2	0	4
Exceeds Expectations	0	0	0	0
Gathers Facts				
Novice	2	1	0	3
In Progress	4	2	4	10
Meets Expectations	1	4	1	6
Exceeds Expectations	0	0	0	0
Brainstorms Solutions				
Novice	1	0	5	6
In Progress	5	4	0	9
Meets Expectations	1	3	0	4
Exceeds Expectations	0	0	0	0
Evaluates				
Novice	5	7	0	12
In Progress	1	0	2	3
Meets Expectations	1	0	3	4
Exceeds Expectations	0	0	0	0
Persistence				
Novice	1	1	0	2
In Progress	4	2	2	8
Meets Expectations	2	4	3	9
Exceeds Expectations	0	0	0	0
Communication				
Novice	5	2	0	7
In Progress	0	2	2	4
Meets Expectations	1	1	1	3
Exceeds Expectations	1	2	2	5

I stared at it for a long time. What does it tell me about my teaching? What does it tell me about my students? How can I use it to inform parents? I can see that I have more thinking to do about assessment.

CHAPTER 3

Show and Tell

My primary English-as-a-Second-Language (ESL) students love mathematics and, for the most part, do well with it. When they begin school, these children speak little, if any, English. I teach in a multigrade class where students in first through fourth grades work and learn together. My overall goals in mathematics are that students progress at their own individual rates and engage in learning at levels that both challenge them and allow for success. For example, a student may work on third-grade mathematics while participating in first-grade writing.

ASSESSING STUDENT PERFORMANCE

Several weeks ago, I reviewed students' work that I had collected during a unit on subtraction. As I read the work, my mind was flooded with many questions and emotions. I realized that the students' written work did not tell the entire story of their mathematics learning—in this instance, borrowing in subtraction. These children, for the most part, were able to work through the problem successfully but sometimes had difficulty expressing their problem-solving strategies.

For example, Alisse can explain borrowing very clearly, as well as her thinking process while she did the work. She can express herself both verbally and in written form. (See **fig. 3.16**.)

FIG. 3.16

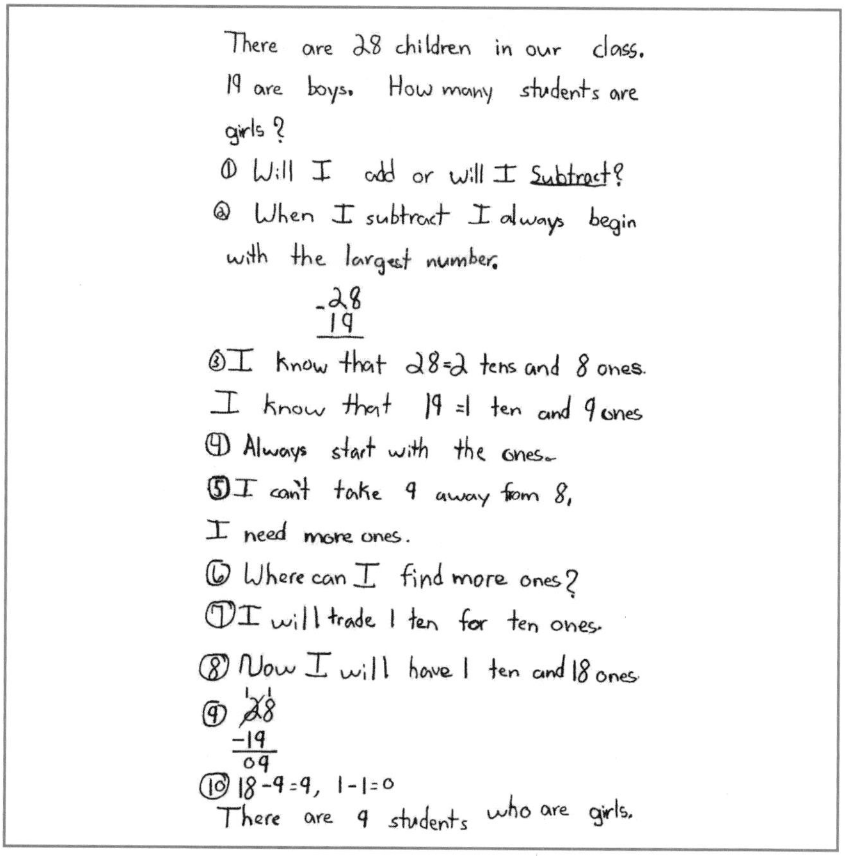

There are 28 children in our class. 19 are boys. How many students are girls?

① Will I add or will I Subtract?

② When I subtract I always begin with the largest number.

$$\begin{array}{r} -28 \\ \underline{19} \end{array}$$

③ I know that 28 = 2 tens and 8 ones. I know that 19 = 1 ten and 9 ones

④ Always start with the ones.

⑤ I can't take 9 away from 8, I need more ones.

⑥ Where can I find more ones?

⑦ I will trade 1 ten for ten ones.

⑧ Now I will have 1 ten and 18 ones

⑨ $\begin{array}{r} 2\!\!\!/8 \\ \underline{-19} \\ 09 \end{array}$

⑩ 18 - 9 = 9, 1 - 1 = 0
There are 9 students who are girls.

Show and Tell

Ricardo, however, has difficulty writing down the steps, but he understands the process. He is very successful in working through the problems in an abstract form. (See **fig. 3.17**.)

FIG. 3.17

There are 28 children in our class. 19 are boys. How many students are girls?

① Will I add or will I <u>subtract?</u>

 I like using patterns

$$-\overset{\frown}{1}\overset{\frown}{8} \quad \overset{\frown}{28} \quad \overset{\frown}{38} \quad -\overset{\frown}{1}\overset{\frown}{8} \quad \overset{\frown}{28} \quad \overset{\frown}{38}$$
$$\frac{-9}{9} \quad \frac{-9}{19} \quad \frac{-9}{28} \quad \frac{-9}{9} \quad \frac{-19}{9} \quad \frac{-19}{19}$$

9 students are girls.

CHAPTER *3*

Show and Tell

Lindy tends to use manipulatives or a picture or diagram to help her solve the problem. (See **fig. 3.18**.)

FIG. 3.18

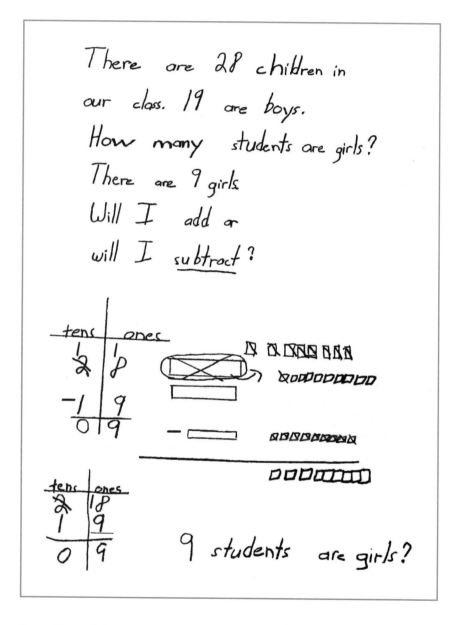

Regardless of the strategy selected to solve a problem, all three children understand the concept.

Show and Tell

I stopped reading the papers and reflected on how most of my students love to use manipulatives and work in small groups. Brainstorming, sharing, and dialogue are important features of my mathematics lessons, and since the beginning of the year, my students had really improved their vocabulary and ability to express their thoughts. Many now resist working individually and dislike paper-and-pencil assignments. Others, however, still prefer to work independently and work with symbols rather than with manipulatives; they are often frustrated by the use of manipulatives and the social interactions necessary for group work. Some don't like "doing math" without symbols and are reluctant to express their thoughts without having the vocabulary to express them clearly.

ACCOUNTABILITY

My thoughts then turned to accountability. How can I share this information with parents? What is it that the parents really want to know? Do they want to know how well their children are achieving compared to other children in our class?

I read through one of the rubrics that the students and I had written together for a unit on subtraction (See **fig. 3.19**).

FIG. 3.19

GRADES 1 AND 2 MATH RUBRIC FOR BORROWING IN SUBTRACTION

4 **AWESOME!**
- Students are busy and on task.
- Students demonstrate a strong understanding of when and how to borrow when subtracting.
- Students can solve problems correctly.
- Students can explain the process to another student, using more than one method.

3 **TERRIFIC!**
- Students are busy and on task.
- Students have a pretty good understanding of when and how to borrow when subtracting.
- Students can usually solve a problem correctly.
- Students have difficulty explaining the process.

2 **OKAY**
- Students are busy and on task.
- Students are not always sure of when and how to borrow when subtracting.
- Students can sometimes solve a problem correctly.
- Students cannot explain the process but they can show how to borrow with pictures or manipulatives.

1 **OOPS**
- Students are busy and on task.
- Students always need help to know when and how to borrow when subtracting.
- Students seldom solve a problem correctly.
- Students cannot explain or show the process.

CHAPTER 3

Show and Tell

The skill checklists, the anecdotal records I have written thus far, and the students' portfolios provide clear evidence of how my students have grown and how different they are. I thought to myself that I could share these pieces of information with parents. I was worried, however, that it might be "information overload" for them. Why was I becoming obsessed with the issue of parent accountability? My students and I know how well they are doing.

I wondered if it was time to involve my students more actively in sharing what they knew and could do. Could they handle the responsibility? I decided to ask my students how we can best show their parents the progress they are making. A most interesting conversation evolved as we brainstormed together:

Teacher: I need your help. Does anyone have an idea on how we can best show your parents your successes in math?

Ricardo: Let us tell them!

Allise: Why can't we show them? Then they'll really understand.

James: We have to make them feel good! Parents don't like to hear bad things.

Teacher: Those are all exciting ideas. We could tell your parents, or we could show your parents. I think you're right, James. Your parents like to feel good when they hear about the work you are doing at school.

Heidi: My mom and dad don't read English very well, so they don't like to read about what I do at school. They like me to show them what I have learned. Sometimes I don't know how to show them. I can't remember all the steps, but I can tell them the answer.

Lindy: Could our parents come to school—even when it's not time for interviews?

Teacher: You are full of good ideas. Can anyone think of why we shouldn't invite your parents to come and visit us at school?

Ricardo: My mom and dad are too busy during the day to come to school. But they are home at night.

Heidi: I think my mom could come in the morning.

Lindy: My dad could come to school during dinnertime. He walks right by our school every day at dinnertime.

Teacher: I think you have some excellent ideas! I will think of a way for us to share your work with your parents in person. Thank you for your help.

Show and Tell

A NEW CONFERENCE STRATEGY

ZAP! It was as though a bolt of lightening had struck me. Once again my ESL students had provided the answers. I felt their suggestions were worth a try. After a brief discussion with my principal, I received permission for our "show and tell" approach.

I sent a letter home asking parents if they would please arrange a time to meet with their child and me for a show-and-tell conference. I gave them a variety of choices—before school, during lunch hour, immediately after school, or three evenings a week. The scheduling became somewhat of a nightmare. After many telephone calls and rescheduling, however, we finally scheduled a time for everyone.

I felt confident that these conferences would allow parents to better understand what their children were learning in school and the progress they were making. The children were enthusiastic and excited. We discussed what they would share with their parents. They began in earnest to prepare.

I am getting nervous now. Next week, our show-and-tell conferences will begin. I still wrestle with many unresolved issues. Have I done the right thing? Did I let the children's enthusiasm cloud my judgment? Hopefully answers will come over the next few weeks.

CHAPTER 3

Student-Led Conferences

I remember Natasha. She was a student in my first-grade class who required special attention. Natasha was frequently absent from school, causing her to miss many important lessons. If Natasha's mother thought that Natasha was not making progress, she called a parent conference—often it seemed with the intention of challenging my teaching. I dreaded the meetings and looked for the warning signs of "impending danger"—her mom's appearance just before the close of a school day or lengthy notes requesting a meeting with her. I found that during these conferences, my competence and professionalism were often challenged.

CONFERENCES WITH NATASHA'S MOTHER

During these interactions with Natasha's mother, I felt that I was being held accountable for those things over which I had little or no control. To protect myself, I documented my work with Natasha and collected evidence of her work. My documentation included my parent communication log, a portfolio of Natasha's work, grid sheets with anecdotal notes about mathematics progress, records of reading and writing conferences, involvement with peers, and special instruction from others. I just knew, however, that Natasha's mother would not be satisfied and that we would make little progress in the meeting. I always felt defensive going into the conferences and always experienced a sense of defeat after they were over.

CONFERENCES WITH NATHAN'S PARENTS

Conversely, thoughts of a conference with Nathan's parents were pleasant and exciting. Nathan was also a student in my first-grade class. His parents were caring and involved, and they viewed me as a partner who contributed greatly to Nathan's educational development. Reviewing their son's portfolio was exciting and rewarding for all of us. All of Nathan's work was completed; it demonstrated his high level of knowledge and skill. His commitment and eagerness to learn were apparent in each product. I knew that my professional skills were recognized and valued by Nathan's parents.

Student-Led Conferences

AN ALTERNATIVE PARENT CONFERENCE

The contrasts between the two conferences were remarkable. I prepared for both in the same way, by gathering student work and making anecdotal notes. I felt my goal for each conference was twofold: to tell parents how well their child was progressing and to explain my learning goals. My planning for Natasha's conference was lonely, painful, and uncertain because her mom was often oppositional and blaming. My session with Nathan's parents was a delightful and rewarding experience because they were supportive and appreciative.

I began to wonder, "Were the conferences with these parents for my benefit, my students' benefit, or their parents' benefit? Did I need to celebrate my students' success and achievement, or did I need a professional pat on the back?" As I reflected on these questions, I began to consider some changes in the way I conducted conferences with parents.

My first step in changing parent conferences was to move to three-way conferences. I wanted students present while the parents and I discussed their progress and made plans. Students were invited to listen to portions of the conversation, to ask questions, and to share briefly. This initial design of the three-way conferences, however, did not permit significant contributions from the students. The limited, voluntary participation of some students revealed to me that first graders can and should be responsible for their own learning.

By involving the children in these conferences, I was able to catch a glimpse of how children naturally assess their own performance and how they might assume responsibility for their own learning. I decided to take another step in involving students further in conferences. Why not have the students lead the conferences? Maybe conferences could evolve from exhausting drudgery to pleasant, profitable experiences that would have an impact on the climate of our classroom and the quality of learning that occurs there.

PREPARING FOR THE CONFERENCES

I began by having my students develop portfolios to be shared at the parent conferences. At the close of each day for the first month of school, the students selected their favorite products for their portfolios. At first, they chose work related primarily to the visual appeal of the product, "My numbers all turn the right way." "My picture of the number story is neat." Later in the year, they chose work related more to learning targets or goals—"I added all of the story problems just right. I know because I checked them with a calculator." "The pattern block puzzle I made caused me to think a long time about how to turn the shapes." I also planned specific products to go into the portfolio. These pieces reflected the various strands of the mathematics curriculum, benchmarks for first grade, and goals set by the school system.

CHAPTER 3

Student-Led Conferences

On the day prior to our first student-led conferences, the students reviewed the work in their portfolios and selected specific pieces to share with their parents. I developed two broad criteria for the selection process:

- The four core content areas must be represented among the pieces selected: mathematics, science, social studies, and communication skills.

- The students must be able to cite a rationale for each piece in the porfolio, and that rationale must be related to the expectations for the content area.

As we reviewed their work, the students discussed their selections with one another and with me, sharing information that I neither knew nor remembered. Much to my surprise, the children understood and could discuss what they had learned as well as the struggles they had experienced during the process.

The true value of each learning event and task was revealed to me as the students discussed what they "took away" from each. Grabbing my faithful clipboard, I made notes about what was and was not effective through the eyes of these students. I also observed that it was as difficult for students to discard certain work as it was for me to do so. Each piece had its own contribution to make to the child's mathematical development.

My excitement about the upcoming student-led conferences reached a crescendo. I envisioned students enthusiastically greeting parents. I could see parents reading the letter that gives an overview of the process and some guiding considerations for the conference. I could see parents reading the captions attached to each selection that describe the context of the task and asking questions of their child. I could anticipate interesting questions and comments from certain parents. I also wondered how Natasha's mother would react to these conferences. Would this new format improve our conferences together?

The challenges were apparent. There was a level of uncertainty with the students in control. Students could represent well what was happening in the classroom and their own performance, or they could misrepresent them. I probably needed to help my students develop a more mature view of themselves, of learning, and of their responsibility for both. How would I support children whose parents did not come for conferences? And, perhaps most important, would these conferences do what I had hoped—prove to be a better model of, and contribute to, the learning in my classroom?

Chapter 4

Facilitator Guidelines and Notes

Guidelines for Facilitating Cases

Using cases to conduct professional development activities requires that a leader, or facilitator, assume a very specific role. The facilitator's role is to ensure that discussions are rich and that issues are addressed in an open, constructive way.

In leading case discussions, facilitators will often need to ask the group to clarify issues to ensure understanding and to encourage opinions and solutions. It is not the role of facilitators to endorse or promote particular beliefs or opinions but, instead, to help participants come to informed conclusions. They must be aware of the needs of the group, be knowledgeable about the issues embedded in the cases, and be prepared to keep discussions moving along a productive track. Discussions must not become negative toward the author, nor should they dwell on a issue or concern that is important only to a very small segment of the group.

Following these general suggestions, we provide here a set of specific facilitator notes for each case. These notes provide a synopsis of the case, a list of issues we believe to be embedded in the case, and a set of questions to promote reflection and discussion about the issues. The notes also include connections to the *Practical Handbooks* of the Classroom Assessment for School Mathematics series and a list of readings pertaining to the issues raised in the case.

Despite these specific notes, facilitating cases will be a challenge. It has been our experience that no two discussions about the same case are exactly alike. We have found that teachers raise many other issues than those listed in the facilitator notes. Our best advice is to be flexible, but focused, in facilitating discussions about cases.

We offer additional advice below to help in preparing for facilitating case discussions and dealing with facilitation dilemmas.

HOW DO I PREPARE FOR FACILITATING CASE DISCUSSIONS?

A key to leading productive discussions about cases is preparation. Before the group meets to discuss the case, we suggest the following preparatory steps:

- Read the case at least twice. Each time write down the main issues that come to mind as you read the case. For each issue, write questions or comments that you might have. Think about how you feel about the issues raised in the case.

- If the case includes students' work, study it carefully. Try to make sense of what the student was thinking during the work. Do any mathematics work included in the case yourself.

- Read through the Facilitator Notes of the case. Compare your issues with those raised in the notes.

- If you do not feel knowledgeable about the terms or issues in the case, use the references cited at the end of the case to do further reading or discuss the terms or issues with a colleague.

- If appropriate and possible, ask participants to complete the "Prereading Activity" in the Facilitator Notes.

Guidelines for Facilitating Cases

HOW DO I SELECT CASES FOR PROFESSIONAL DEVELOPMENT ACTIVITIES OR CLASSES?

Consider the needs of participants of the case discussion (e.g., Do teachers want to learn how to develop tasks? Do teachers want to learn how to score open-ended tasks? Do teachers want to learn how to create rubrics?). Also consider the context in which the case is being presented (e.g., Has a new state assessment system been mandated? Do teachers in a school want to change or reach consensus about assessment practices? Do teachers agree on assessment approaches?). Think about how you will make sure the needs and context are addressed in the discussions.

HOW DO I LEAD DISCUSSIONS ABOUT THE CASES?

- If possible, distribute the case before the case discussion meeting so that participants can read and reflect on it.

- Begin the session by informing participants about the purpose of the discussion and the type of climate that you hope to achieve together. This means ensuring that all opinions and ideas are discussed openly and respectfully. Tell participants that your role is to help them examine alternative ideas carefully. Be careful about offering your own opinion or resolution.

- Ask all participants to read the case silently. Make sure they have had ample opportunity to read the case entirely.

- Encourage participants to take notes as they read. Simply suggest that they may want to write down their thoughts as they read the case.

- Have participants work in pairs to decide some of the issues raised in the case.

- As issues and dilemmas are raised, ask questions to help participants clarify those issues and dilemmas. (See Facilitator Notes for examples of these questions.)

- For large groups, consider having groups of three or four participants discuss what issues they see in the case before beginning large-group discussion. Smaller groups give every participant a chance to express his or her thoughts or opinions.

- Stimulate discussion by asking general questions like:

  - What facts do we know from the case?
  - What issues came to mind as you read this case?
  - What dilemmas arose for this teacher?
  - What is this case about?

Guidelines for Facilitating Cases

- Sometimes participants will want to jump immediately to a solution to the problem or dilemma. Keep the discussion focused initially on developing a sound analysis of the problem before attempting to solve it. When participants begin solving too early, ask questions like "What does Joe say or do that leads you to that interpretation?"

- Once an issue or dilemma is identified, probe for further discussion about it. Ask for opinions about the issue or possible resolutions to the dilemmas. Make sure everyone who wants to speak has a chance to do so.

- A visual record of the conversation can be helpful. Using a flip chart, overhead transparencies, or a white board helps keep track of the conversation.

- As the discussion winds down, bring some sort of closure to the discussion. "How might the teacher in the case resolve the dilemma? How might this dilemma be avoided in the future?"

- If participants fail to raise an important issue or dilemma, you might say, "What do you think about ...?" to raise it for them.

- Close the session with a debriefing of the discussions and perhaps a plan for next steps.

WHAT PROBLEMS MIGHT ARISE DURING CASE DISCUSSIONS AND HOW DO I HANDLE THEM?

In facilitating group discussions, challenges may arise. Some participants may not speak, whereas others may speak too frequently. Some participants may speak derogatorily about others. Some participants may espouse beliefs and practices about which you disagree. *Exploring Classroom Assessment in Mathematics* by Deborah Bryant and Mark Driscoll (1998) and *A Guide to Facilitating Cases in Education* by Barbara Miller and Ilene Kantrov (1998b) offer specific suggestions to resolve facilitation dilemmas. Some of the suggestions that follow were adapted from their advice.

If the participants expect something else from the professional development experience than discussions about cases ...

Talk about the two sets of needs openly. Offer them a compromise by giving them some of what they want in addition to discussing cases. For example, if teachers want to learn to create rubrics, do so before or after discussing a case about dilemmas that arise from creating rubrics.

CHAPTER *4*

Guidelines for Facilitating Cases

If a small group of teachers comes to the session with a specific agenda in mind …

Listen carefully to their concerns, acknowledge them, and discuss them openly with the whole group. Work their agenda into subsequent discussions about issues and dilemmas.

If a participant is reluctant to speak or a participant tends to dominate the discussion …

Divide the group into smaller groups of two to four participants. Give members of the smaller group two minutes to say what they wish. Keep time carefully and require that other participants listen carefully without responding. Ask groups to summarize the issues and dilemmas raised in the discussions.

If participants begin to speak derogatorily of the teacher in the case, another individual, or other individuals …

Focus the discussion on why the teacher or individuals might have done what they did. Are there legitimate reasons for their behaviors? What factors might have caused them to do what they did? Or, focus the discussion on solutions to the dilemmas rather than on blame. Discuss what the teacher or individuals might have done differently.

If a participant makes a comment with which you strongly disagree or that is not in line with current thinking on the issue …

Give other participants a chance to respond to the comment. Explore everyone's beliefs about the comment and ask them to provide reasons for their beliefs. Use the comments as a chance to conduct an experiment from the disagreement. For example, suppose a participant comments that writing in mathematics is a waste of time. Ask how the participants might conduct an experiment to see if writing in mathematics classes improves students' mathematical understanding or abilities.

NOTES FOR
"The Power of the Blank Page"

CASE SYNOPSIS

A first-grade teacher finds a stack of booklets containing blank pages except for numerals written in the corner of each page. Her students reveal different ways of thinking about numbers in their discussions of ways to fill out the blank pages. Bothered that her current assessment practices fail to reveal this rich kind of mathematical thinking, she wonders how she might better assess her students' understanding.

PREREADING ACTIVITY

Discuss what it means for students to understand the concepts of addition, subtraction, multiplication, and division. What questions might teachers ask to determine if students truly understand these operations?

MAIN ASSESSMENT ISSUES

- Changing assessment practices
- Assessing students' thinking and understanding
- Assessing students' beliefs and attitudes
- Improving teaching through classroom assessment

DISCUSSION NOTES AND QUESTIONS

Changing Assessment Practices

Making Changes ... After recognizing that her students were quite creative in thinking about numbers, the teacher lamented that her current assessment practices did not seem to capture this thinking. What specific assessment approaches might the teacher use to assess students' number understanding?

Resources ... The teacher seemed to want to change her assessment practices. What advice would you give a teacher who wishes to change assessment practices? What resources are available to help the teacher make such a change?

Assessing Student Thinking

Joan's Multiplication ... Joan developed a subtraction strategy to create ones. What might a teacher infer about Joan's understanding of numbers and operations on the basis of her comments and work?

Frank's Division ... Frank learned about division from his buddy. What might a teacher infer about his understanding of numbers and operations on the basis of Frank's comments and work?

Alisha's Letters ... With some prompting from her teacher, Alisha uses names to make numbers. What might a teacher infer about her understanding of numbers and operations from Alisha's comments and work? How might a teacher help Alisha feel more positive about working with numbers?

CHAPTER *4*

NOTES FOR
"The Power of the Blank Page"

Assessing Beliefs and Attitudes

The students had a wide range of beliefs and attitudes about mathematics and numbers, in particular. What were some of them? How did their beliefs and attitudes affect their work in the number booklets? What systematic assessment strategies might be used to capture their beliefs and attitudes more specifically?

Improving Teaching Through Classroom Assessment

What Next? ... The teacher wonders how she can improve her teaching after watching and listening to her students. What might a teacher do as follow-up activities with Joan, Frank, and Alisha? How might teachers address the range of thinking illustrated by Joan, Frank, and Alisha?

CONNECTIONS TO THE *PRACTICAL HANDBOOKS*

Topic	Handbook	Section
Changing assessment practices	K-2 Handbook	Why Is It Important to Assess?
	3-5 Handbook	Changing Assessment Practices
Assessing thinking and understanding	K-2 Handbook	Assessing Students' Understanding of Mathematical Concepts
		Assessing Mathematical Processes
	3-5 Handbook	Defining and Using Standards in Assessment
Assessing beliefs and attitudes	K-2 Handbook	Assessing Students' Attitudes about Mathematics
Improving teaching through assessment	3-5 Handbook	Program Evaluation

SUGGESTIONS FOR FURTHER READING

Bright, George. "Understanding Children's Reasoning." *Teaching Children Mathematics* 3 (September 1996): 18–22.

Collison, Judith. "Using Performance Assessment to Determine Mathematics Dispositions." *Arithmetic Teacher* 39 (February 1992): 40–47.

Cross, Lee, and Michael Hynes. "Assessing Mathematics Learning for Students with Learning Differences." *Arithmetic Teacher* 41 (March 1994): 371–77.

D'Aboy, Diana. "Assessment through Incredible Equations." *Teaching Children Mathematics* 4 (October 1997): 76–80.

Moon, Jean C. "Connecting Learning and Teaching through Assessment." *Arithmetic Teacher* 41 (September 1993): 13–15.

NOTES FOR
"On-the-Job Learning"

CASE SYNOPSIS

At a workshop, a first-grade teacher is introduced to the importance of recording classroom observation notes on students' understanding. The teacher likes the idea and decides to try it in her classroom. She is challenged, however, by the complexities in creating such a system. She struggles to create a system that is manageable and is true to her original goal of capturing students' thinking and understanding. She finds that she needs to make adjustments in her original approach. She wonders how many students she should observe each day, in what form she should record her observations, and what kinds of notes she should take. In the end, she is left wondering how to capture learning moments for students who are not on her list for a particular day, how to help students feel comfortable with her observations and note-taking, and how to best share the information she collected with parents and, perhaps, students.

PREREADING ACTIVITY

Option 1

Answer the following questions as an individual writing task:

- ■ "How do (would) you record or use observations of students in your classroom?"
- ■ "What are the strengths and weaknesses of this system?"
- ■ "When you observe, listen to, or question students, what is your purpose?"

Share your responses with others.

Option 2

Divide participants in groups of four and have three of them work a mathematics problem. Ask the fourth participant to record the participants' thinking and understanding as they work the problem. Discuss what guidelines they used in recording their group members' thinking and what thinking they captured. Have observers comment on their experience as observers: Was it difficult to keep track of the various groups? Did they take notes? How did they organize their notes? What was challenging about observing? What was rewarding?

MAIN ASSESSMENT ISSUES

- ■ Recording classroom observation data
- ■ Establishing a clear purpose for assessment

CHAPTER *4*

NOTES FOR
"On-the-Job Learning"

DISCUSSION NOTES AND QUESTIONS

Recording Classroom Data

Initial Attempts ... The teacher described her initial attempts at keeping records of her observations of the students in her first-grade classroom. What challenges did she encounter? What resources might help her overcome the initial challenges?

Struggling with the System ... The teacher worked hard to establish a viable system. Why was it so important to get the details of the process right? What were some of strategies she tried? What other strategies might she try? What are other strategies for capturing students' thinking and understanding?

Establishing a Clear Purpose

A Clear Purpose ... As the teacher refined her system, she asked herself, "Why am I keeping records in the first place?" What do you think the teacher's purpose for creating this system was? Did her purpose change? If so, how? How might establishing a clear purpose help in developing a viable assessment system?

What to Do Next ... At the end of the case, the teacher reflected on some of the challenges she still faced in recording observation notes for students. What were those challenges? What do you think she might do next to resolve those challenges? What advice would you give this teacher?

CONNECTIONS TO THE *PRACTICAL HANDBOOKS*

Topic	Handbook	Section
Recording classroom observation data	*K-2 Handbook*	Conversations, Interviews, and Observations
	3-5 Handbook	Questions, Observations, Interviews, and Conferences
		Documenting Assessment Results
Establishing a purpose for assessment	*K-2 Handbook*	Why Is It Important to Assess?
	3-5 Handbook	Making Assessment Plans

SUGGESTIONS FOR FURTHER READING

Clarke, David J. "Activating Assessment Alternatives in Mathematics." *Arithmetic Teacher* 39 (February 1992): 24–29.

Cole, Karen A. "Walking Around: Getting More from Informal Assessment." *Mathematics Teaching in the Middle Grades* 4 (January 1999): 224–27.

Cross, Lee, and Michael Hynes. "Assessing Mathematics Learning for Students with Learning Differences." *Arithmetic Teacher* 41 (March 1994): 371–77.

Stenmark, Jean, ed. *Mathematics Assessment: Myths, Models, Good Questions, and Practical Suggestions.* Reston, Va.: National Council of Teachers of Mathematics, 1991.

NOTES FOR

"How Do I Assess Thee? Let Me Count the Ways ..."

CASE SYNOPSIS

A fourth- and fifth-grade ESL teacher with seventeen years experience decides to change assessment practices after taking a college course that focused on classroom assessment. She establishes a monthly schedule to use Problems of the Week (POWs), performance tasks, investigations, and journal writing. After several months and complaints from students, she wonders what she has learned about her students and if she has tried to do too much.

PREREADING ACTIVITY

Discuss what mathematics abilities (e.g., problem solving, proficiency, understanding, communication, reasoning) might be assessed in elementary classrooms. After generating a list of abilities, discuss appropriate tools and approaches for assessing them.

MAIN ASSESSMENT ISSUES

- Setting goals and communicating expectations about assessment
- Creating and managing an assessment system
- Interpreting multiple sources of assessment

DISCUSSION NOTES AND QUESTIONS

Setting Goals and Expectations

Setting Goals ... Stimulated by a college course, the teacher decided to use a variety of assessment approaches after years of teaching, learning, and practice using the NCTM *Curriculum and Evaluation Standards for School Mathematics*. What changes did she make? What issues or concerns might have motivated her to make these changes? What do you think her goals for assessment and instruction were? How important is it to have explicit goals for assessment?

Communicating Expectations ... The teacher clearly had high expectations for her students' mathematical performance. In reviewing the assessment tasks and the students' work, what expectations did she have for her students' mathematical performance? How did she communicate her expectations to her students? What other ways might teachers communicate assessment expectations to students?

Creating and Managing an Assessment System

An Organized Assessment System ... The teacher developed an assessment system that used POWs one week, performance tasks the next week, investigations the third week, and journal writing the final week. What are the advantages and disadvantages of a structured system like this? In what other ways might teachers develop systems that include a variety of tools and approaches?

CHAPTER *4*

NOTES FOR
"How Do I Assess Thee?
Let Me Count the Ways ..."

Too Much Too Fast ... After several months, the teacher was concerned that she had tried to do too much with her assessment. How much change in assessment is *too much*? How can teachers use multiple assessments, as advocated by NCTM, in a realistic, manageable way? What factors influence how much change teachers can accomplish in their assessment practices? What strategies might help teachers make changes in their assessment practices?

Interpreting Assessment Results

Assessing Progress ... The teacher had difficulty in assessing her students' progress with her system. She was not sure that she had successfully gathered enough information about each child. Are her concerns valid? Why or why not? What other assessment systems might teachers use to assess student progress?

Too Much Information ... The teacher was overwhelmed by the amount of information that she had gathered about each student. She was not sure what to do with the results of her assessment system. In what ways might teachers organize the results of assessment in order to help them communicate student results effectively?

CONNECTIONS TO THE *PRACTICAL HANDBOOKS*

Topic	Handbook	Section
Setting assessment goals and expectations	*3-5 Handbook*	Defining and Using Standards in Assessment
Creating and managing a system	*K-2 Handbook*	Conversations, Interviews, and Observations
	3-5 Handbook	Selecting and Developing Assessment Tools: What Are My Choices?
		Managing Time and Logistics
Interpreting multiple sources of assessment	K-2 Handbook	Report Cards
	3-5 Handbook	Looking at Students' Work

SUGGESTIONS FOR FURTHER READING

Clarke, David J. "Activating Assessment Alternatives in Mathematics." *Arithmetic Teacher* 39 (February 1992): 24–29.

Lambdin, Diana V., and Clare Forseth. "Seamless Assessment/Instruction = Good Teaching." *Teaching Children Mathematics* 2 (January 1996): 294–98.

Sammons, Kay, Beth Kobett, Joan Heiss, and Francis (Skip) Fennell. "Linking Instruction and Assessment in the Mathematics Classroom." *Arithmetic Teacher* 39 (February 1992): 11–16.

NOTES FOR
"Primary Portfolios"

CASE SYNOPSIS

A primary school teacher chooses to have her students compile mathematics portfolios to prepare them for the state assessment. After attending workshops and experimenting with portfolios, she finds that the portfolios help her students learn mathematics. Although she values portfolios as an assessment approach, she struggles with managing them and finding good tasks for her students.

PREREADING ACTIVITY

■ Discuss what mathematics portfolios for primary school students (K–3) might look like.

■ Discuss different types of mandated state or province assessment programs in the United States and Canada. How are they alike and how are they different?

MAIN ASSESSMENT ISSUES

■ Implementing state-mandated assessments in the classroom

■ Finding and creating good assessment tasks

■ Using portfolios for classroom assessment

■ Dealing with the difficulty of balanced assessment

DISCUSSION NOTES AND QUESTIONS

State-Mandated Assessment

Teacher Reaction ... The teacher changed her assessment practices because of a state-mandated assessment system. She began to use mathematics portfolios because the state required them of all fourth-grade students. The teacher seemed to adopt the new assessment approach with enthusiasm. What factors might have influenced her enthusiasm? What other reactions might teachers have to state-mandated assessment? What factors might influence these reactions?

Preparing Students for State-Mandated Assessment ... The state-mandated assessment for mathematics included open-ended questions, group performance events, and portfolios. Beyond using these assessment approaches in their classroom assessment, what else might teachers do to improve student performance on these types of assessment?

CHAPTER *4*

NOTES FOR
"Primary Portfolios"

Finding and Creating Good Assessment Tasks

Flexible Tasks ... The teacher had difficulty finding and creating tasks that were suitable for six-, seven- and eight-year-olds. Can one task assess mathematics competence at different grade levels? Give reasons or examples for your response. How might teachers assess learners of different ages and abilities? How might a teacher develop an assessment system in a multiage classroom?

Good Tasks ... The teacher had difficulty finding good tasks. What did this teacher mean by *good tasks*? In your opinion, what constitutes a good assessment task? What criteria might be used to determine whether tasks are good or appropriate?

Resources for Tasks ... The teacher finally decided to create her own tasks and rubrics. What must a teacher consider in developing good tasks and rubrics? What resources might help elementary school teachers develop good tasks and rubrics? Where might elementary school teachers find good examples of tasks and rubrics for their students?

Using Portfolios for Mathematics Assessment

Portfolios as an Assessment Tool ...The teacher identified several advantages and disadvantages in using portfolios to assess mathematics performance in the elementary school grades. What were they? What are other advantages and disadvantages? What different purposes might mathematics portfolios address? What mathematics abilities might portfolios be used to assess?

Managing Portfolios ... The teacher had some difficulty in managing the mathematics portfolios of all her students. What strategies might teachers use to manage portfolios effectively? What resources might help teachers manage the portfolio process?

Dealing with the Difficulty of Balanced Assessment

The teacher's closing remark in the case was "The more I learn about my students, the more I realize how hard really good assessment is." What do you think she meant by this remark? Provide some personal examples of how difficult really good assessment is. What is so hard about good assessment?

NOTES FOR
"Primary Portfolios"

CONNECTIONS TO THE *PRACTICAL HANDBOOKS*

Topic	Handbook	Section
Implementing state-mandated assessments	*3-5 Handbook*	Assessment beyond the Classroom
Finding and creating assessment tasks	*K-2 Handbook*	Performance Assessment and Tasks
	3-5 Handbook	Tasks and Open-Ended Questions
		Evaluating Assessment Tasks
Using portfolios for classroom assessment	*K-2 Handbook*	Portfolios
	3-5 Handbook	Portfolios and Collections of Work
		Managing Portfolios
Dealing with balanced assessment	*3-5 Handbook*	Selecting and Developing Assessment Tools: What Are My Choices?
		Managing Time and Logistics

SUGGESTIONS FOR FURTHER READING

Collison, Judith. "Using Performance Assessment to Determine Mathematics Dispositions." *Arithmetic Teacher* 39 (February 1992): 40–47.

Lambdin, Diana V., and Vicki L. Walker. "Planning for Classroom Portfolio Assessment." *Arithmetic Teacher* 41 (February 1994): 318–24.

Schoenfeld, Alan, Hugh Burkhardt, Phil Daro, Jim Ridgway, Judah Schwartz, and Sandra Wilcox. *Balanced Assessment: Elementary Grades Assessment Package 1.* White Plains, N.Y.: Dale Seymour Publications, 1999.

———. *Balanced Assessment: Elementary Grades Assessment Package 2.* White Plains, N.Y.: Dale Seymour Publications, 1999.

Sullivan, Peter, and David Clarke. "Catering to All Abilities through 'Good Questions.'" *Arithmetic Teacher* 39 (October 1991): 14–18.

Zawojewski, Judith. "Polishing a Data Task: Seeking Better Assessment." *Teaching Children Mathematics* 2 (February 1996): 372–78.

NOTES FOR
"When the Wrong Way Works"

CASE SYNOPSIS

A fifth-grade teacher is puzzled by the performance of some of his students on a mathematics quiz involving subtraction of fractions. The students report doing well on practice problems but use inappropriate strategies for solving problems on the quiz. He interviews them in class to find out more about their thinking and discovers a misunderstanding about the algorithm for subtraction of fractions. Furthermore, he discovers that the inappropriate strategy the students have been using worked for all of the problems on the "practice test" he provided for students. He is left wondering how to correct their misconceptions and how to make the practice test serve as a better diagnostic tool.

PREREADING ACTIVITY

Work through the three problems on the teacher's "practice test" in the case. Share your strategies for solving the problems. What problems do students generally have in solving problems like these? What misunderstandings might you anticipate from a class of fifth graders on problems like these?

MAIN ASSESSMENT ISSUES

- Using assessments to make valid inferences about student understanding
- Interviewing students and discussing their thinking to guide instruction
- Responding to a student's misunderstanding

DISCUSSION NOTES AND QUESTIONS

Using Assessments to Make Inferences about Students' Thinking

The Three Examples ... Why did the three examples work the wrong way? What is the general pattern for this situation?

Uncovering Misconceptions ... Why did the practice test fail as a diagnostic assessment? What information did it give the teacher about his students? What were its limitations? How might the practice test be revised to capture the students' understanding of subtracting fractions?

Interviewing Students

The teacher decided to interview students as a group. What was his goal? What kinds of questions did he ask? What are the advantages and disadvantages of using interviews as assessment tools?

NOTES FOR
"When the Wrong Way Works"

Responding to Misunderstandings

Making Corrections ... Once the teacher found that the students did not understand the process, he decided to correct it. What strategies did he use with the group? What strategies might he use with the whole class? What might his next assessment of subtracting fractions look like?

What Next? ... At the end, the teacher is left considering what his next instructional strategy should be to help his students better understand subtracting fractions. What instructional strategies would you suggest? What general recommendations would you make to the teacher about his teaching of fraction subtraction?

CONNECTIONS TO THE *PRACTICAL HANDBOOKS*

Topic	Handbook	Section
Making inferences	*K-2 Handbook*	Assessing Students' Understanding of Mathematical Concepts
	3-5 Handbook	Looking at Students' Work
Interviewing students	*K-2 Handbook*	Conversations, Interviews, and Observations
	3-5 Handbook	Questions, Observations, Interviews, and Conferences
Responding to a student's misunderstanding	*K-2 Handbook*	Assessing Students' Understanding of Mathematical Concepts
	3-5 Handbook	Looking at Students' Work

SUGGESTIONS FOR FURTHER READING

Bright, George. "Understanding Children's Reasoning." *Teaching Children Mathematics* 3 (September 1996): 18–22.

Lankford, Francis G., Jr. "What Can a Teacher Learn about a Pupil's Thinking through Oral Interviews?" *Arithmetic Teacher* 40 (October 1992): 106–11.

Lindquist, Mary M. "Assessing through Questioning." *Arithmetic Teacher* 35 (January 1988): 16–18.

Long, Madeleine J., and Meir Ben-Hur. "Informing Learning through the Clinical Interview." *Arithmetic Teacher* 38 (February 1991): 44–46.

Rowan, Thomas E., and Josepha Robles. "Using Questions to Help Children Build Mathematical Power." *Teaching Children Mathematics* 9 (May 1998): 504–509.

Sammons, Kay, Beth Kobett, Joan Heiss, and Francis (Skip) Fennell. "Linking Instruction and Assessment in the Mathematics Classroom." *Arithmetic Teacher* 39 (February 1992): 11–16.

CHAPTER *4*

NOTES FOR
"A Team Approach"

CASE SYNOPSIS

First-grade teachers Ann, Don, and Tina are participating in a schoolwide project to assess students' problem-solving skills by collecting responses on one problem-solving performance task each quarter. In the first quarter of the year, students' responses vary greatly because of differences in the way the teachers administered the tasks. Consequently, the teachers decide that they need common guidelines to ensure equity and consistency in scoring. As they analyze and score the students' responses on the second task, they reach consensus on most of the work—until they come to Mark's paper. Mark is Ann's student, and Ann, knowing Mark, gives him a higher score than the others do. Don and Tina argue that it is important that the rubric they developed be applied to all students' work in the same way.

PREREADING ACTIVITY

Select a performance task that has a specific rubric and some sample student work. Ask participants to solve the task individually and score the papers according to the rubric. Have them discuss areas of agreement and disagreement. Where did they reach consensus? Where did they disagree and why?

MAIN ASSESSMENT ISSUES

- ■ Establishing a purpose for assessment
- ■ Using criterion-referenced assessments
- ■ Establishing conditions for assessment
- ■ Scoring students' work consistently and reliably

DISCUSSION NOTES AND QUESTIONS

Establishing a Purpose for Assessment

Assessing Progress ... The teachers developed a rubric to score student work. What was the purpose of the rubric? How did the rubric dictate the nature of the students' responses? Ann wanted the rubric to show progress. How might progress be assessed and documented?

What Do Numbers Do? ... What do you think Ann fears when she says "label Mark as a 1 student?" How can assessment labels hurt students? What can be done to humanize records of student achievement?

Using Criterion-Referenced Assessments

Changing the Criteria ... The teachers identified important criteria to be used in judging students' work at the outset. Ann seemed to change the criteria after reviewing Mark's work. What caused her to change her mind?

Sticking to the Criteria ... In discussing Mark's paper, Ann wanted the score to measure Mark's progress as well as his degree of mathematics learning. Don and Tina argued that the agreed-upon rubric provided a standard that did not include progress. Who was right in this discussion? Why was there a difference in interpretation?

NOTES FOR
"A Team Approach"

Establishing Conditions for Assessment

For the first task, the teachers used different materials when administrating the tasks. For the second task, the teachers agreed on the wording of the task and the materials to be used. When might teachers want to vary the conditions under which they give assessment tasks? When might they want to standardize the conditions?

Scoring Student Work Consistently and Reliably

Improving Scoring Strategies ... Ann, Tina, and Don were struggling with scoring papers reliably and consistently, especially when their own students were involved. What strategies might help them improve their scoring consistently?

Mark's Paper ... As the case ended, Ann, Tina, and Don were still in conversation about what to do with Mark's paper. Ann argued that Mark should be recognized for his effort and how far he has come; Tina and Don appeared to be agree that Mark's paper should be rated a 1 on the rubric. What should they do next? Is there a compromise position? What is best for Mark in this situation?

CONNECTIONS TO THE *PRACTICAL HANDBOOKS*

Topic	Handbook	Section
Establishing a purpose	*K-2 Handbook*	Why Is It Important to Assess?
	3-5 Handbook	Making Assessment Plans
Using criterion-referenced assessments	*K-2 Handbook*	Performance Assessment and Tasks
	3-5 Handbook	Scoring and Grading
Establishing conditions for assessment	*3-5 Handbook*	Changing Assessment Practices
Scoring students' work	*K-2 Handbook*	Performance Assessment and Tasks
		Portfolios
	3-5 Handbook	Scoring and Grading

SUGGESTIONS FOR FURTHER READING

Brown-Herbst, Kari. "So Math Isn't Just Answers." *Mathematics Teaching in the Middle School* 4 (April 1999): 448–55.

Conway, Kathleen D. "Assessing Open-Ended Problems." *Mathematics Teaching in the Middle School* 4 (May 1999): 510–14.

Kroll, Diana Lambdin, Joanna O. Masingila, and Sue Tinsley Mau. "Cooperative Problem Solving: But What about Grading?" *Arithmetic Teacher* 39 (February 1992): 17–23.

CHAPTER *4*

NOTES FOR
"If They Only Knew Michael"

CASE SYNOPSIS

As part of a professional development group gaining experience with authentic assessment, a fourth-grade teacher administers an assessment task to her students. She hopes her class will clearly explain the mathematical thinking that they used to arrive at their final solution. Before scoring the students' work, she and her colleagues determine the criteria for sorting the work into two piles. As she scores the work of one of her students, the teacher discovers she has based her score on her personal knowledge of the student. She wonders how she can be "objective" when scoring her own students' work and how she can promote quality work from all of her students.

PREREADING ACTIVITY

Work the task and compare solutions and strategies. Note what each person includes or omits in his or her response.

MAIN ASSESSMENT ISSUES

- ■ Communicating quality-of-work expectations to students
- ■ Designing assessment tasks
- ■ Determining criteria for scoring
- ■ Scoring students' work objectively

DISCUSSION NOTES AND QUESTIONS

Communicating Quality-of-Work Expectations

The teacher was surprised by the fact that many of her students did not write complete explanations of their thinking when solving this task. She hoped they would express the strategy that they used to arrive at their final solution, as well as their final answer. How can teachers convey expectations to students about what constitutes quality writing in mathematics class? When is it appropriate or necessary for students to write out their complete thought process in solving a problem? When might this not be a goal?

Designing Assessment Tasks

The group of teachers hoped that the modifications they made to the original task would encourage students to produce a clear explanation of their thinking. To what extent did the task written by these teachers require students to explain the mathematical thinking the teachers hoped to see? To what extent did the task clearly convey what a complete answer should include? How might this task be revised to require students to show their thinking? How can students know when they have complete answers to tasks?

NOTES FOR

"If They Only Knew Michael"

Determining Criteria for Scoring

Reviewing Student Work ... The assessment group determined the criteria for scoring the student. What do you think about the criteria they set? The teacher says that the group "had agreed to criteria for 'RR' and 'MI' without really discussing in depth what we considered the most important aspects of this task. We evidently were not explicit enough about what 'showing that insufficient funds were remaining to buy more items' meant ..." To what extent is it important to discuss all aspects of a task before scoring it? What process for setting criteria might have clarified the criteria for the scorers? Should the context of scoring, such as for the purpose of teachers' professional development, affect the process?

Modifying Criteria ... The group of teachers decided to modify the criteria for what constituted a complete rationale after seeing that very few students gave complete rationales. What do you think of this decision? What might the teachers have considered when making this decision? When might it be appropriate to alter a criteria in light of the actual results of students' work? When might this not be a good idea?

Scoring Students' Work Objectively

Prior Knowledge ... The teacher was concerned that her knowledge of one student interfered with the score she gave him. Is this a valid concern? What might be the benefits of knowing the student whose paper you are scoring? What might be the disadvantages? When might it be appropriate to "add" knowledge of a student into a score you assign?

Fairness ... Although Michael did not include the total cost of the items he would buy or explicitly state the amount of money he had left over, his teacher believed he knew this and scored his work "Ready for Revision." Following the criteria they have set, the other teachers scored it "More Instruction Needed." What score would you have given Michael? What issues of *fairness* are raised in assigning each score to Michael's paper?

CHAPTER *4*

NOTES FOR
"If They Only Knew Michael"

CONNECTIONS TO THE *PRACTICAL HANDBOOKS*

Topic	Handbook	Section
Communicating expectations to students	*K-2 Handbook*	On a Weekly Basis
	3-5 Handbook	Feedback to Students
Designing assessment tasks	*K-2 Handbook*	Performance Assessment and Tasks
	3-5 Handbook	Developing Good Assessment Tasks
Determining criteria for scoring	*K-2 Handbook*	Performance Assessment and Tasks
	3-5 Handbook	Scoring and Grading
Scoring students' work objectively	*3-5 Handbook*	Scoring and Grading

SUGGESTIONS FOR FURTHER READING

Brown-Herbst, Kari. "So Math Isn't Just Answers." *Mathematics Teaching in the Middle School* 4 (April 1999): 448–55.

Conway, Kathleen D. "Assessing Open-Ended Problems." *Mathematics Teaching in the Middle School* 4 (May 1999): 510–14.

Kroll, Diana Lambdin, Joanna O. Masingila, and Sue Tinsley Mau. "Cooperative Problem Solving: But What about Grading?" *Arithmetic Teacher* 39 (February 1992): 17–23.

Swan, Malcolm. "Assessing Mathematical Processes: The English Experience." *Mathematics Teaching in the Middle School* 1 (March-April 1996): 706–11

NOTES FOR
"Students as Assessors"

CASE SYNOPSIS

A teacher designs a lesson to involve her students in self-assessment. She has them solve a problem in groups, present their solutions to the class, and develop criteria for assessing the group presentations. As she has her students discuss their criteria and assign 100 points to the set, she learns about her students' values about mathematics. She wonders how she can get them to come up with more complex criteria for assessing their work in the future.

PREREADING ACTIVITY

Solve the problem in the case about the Sorcerer's Apprentice. Discuss different approaches that were used to solve the problem.

MAIN ASSESSMENT ISSUES

- Involving students in assessment
- Designing scoring tools
- Helping students value mathematical thinking

DISCUSSION NOTES AND QUESTIONS

Involving Students in Assessment

Having Students Determine Assessment Criteria ... The teacher designed a multistep lesson that began by involving students in cooperatively solving a problem. What type of problem did she use? What might be the benefits of using this type of problem when having students assess their work for the first time? What might be the disadvantages?

Teacher's Role ... The teacher led a discussion in which the students offered suggestions for criteria. What role did she play in this discussion? What other questions might she have posed during this discussion to have students generate the criteria?

Student-Selected Criteria ... The teacher wondered how she can have her students come up with different criteria in the future. What do you think of the criteria the students came up with? What criteria would you like to see students generate when assessing their work? In addition to the process used by this teacher, what processes can teachers use to have students develop assessment criteria?

CHAPTER *4*

"Students as Assessors"

Developing Scoring Tools

Developing a Scoring Sheet ... The teacher combined different criteria from each group into seven final criteria. She asked students to assign a total of 100 points to this set. What do you think about her strategy of having students assign points? What are the advantages of using a score sheet for student assessment? What might be the disadvantages?

Choosing Assessment Tools ... The teacher said that since the students had not yet had experience using rubrics, she wanted them to develop a score sheet. How might she have had them develop a rubric to assess their presentations? If different assessment tools lend themselves to assessing different outcomes, what might be the advantages of having students develop and use a rubric to assess group presentations? What other types of tools might the teacher have had students develop to assess their presentations?

Helping Students Value Mathematics Thinking

Choosing Assessment Targets ... The teacher decided that she wanted her students to assess the groups' presentations as opposed to the groups' solutions to the problem. What might be the difference between assessing these two? What do you think of this decision? Why do you think she began the process of student self-assessment in this way?

Valuing Solution Strategies ... The teacher wanted the students to distinguish between having a solution strategy that leads to a correct answer and having a correct answer. What was the error in the solution from Josh's group? What could be characterized as his group's solution strategy? How might the Sorcerer's Apprentice problem promote this distinction between strategy and answer? How might it not lend itself to promoting this distinction?

The teacher wondered what types of problems will lead her students to value solution strategies as a criterion. She thought that problems that have more than one solution may do this. What do you think of this idea? How would you get students to value different solution strategies when assessing themselves? She also wonders if having them engage in self-assessment using their criteria will help them become better problem solvers. What do you think?

NOTES FOR
"Students as Assessors"

CONNECTIONS TO THE *PRACTICAL HANDBOOKS*

Topic	Handbook	Section
Involving students in assessment	*K-2 Handbook*	Student-Led Conferences
	3-5 Handbook	Student Involvement and Self-Assessment
Designing scoring tools	*K-2 Handbook*	Performance Assessment and Tasks
	3-5 Handbook	Scoring and Grading
Helping students value mathematical thinking	*3-5 Handbook*	Feedback to Students' Thinking
		Helping Students Write in Mathematics
	K–2 Handbook	Assessing Mathematical Processes

SUGGESTIONS FOR FURTHER READING

Brown-Herbst, Kari. "So Math Isn't Just Answers." *Mathematics Teaching in the Middle School* 4 (April 1999): 448–55.

Stenmark, Jean, ed. *Mathematics Assessment: Myths, Models, Good Questions, and Practical Suggestions*. Reston, Va.: National Council of Teachers of Mathematics, 1991.

Tonack, De A. "A Teacher's View of Classroom Assessment: What & How." *Mathematics Teaching in the Middle School* 2 (November-December 1996): 70–78.

CHAPTER *4*

NOTES FOR
"The New Student"

CASE SYNOPSIS

In January, Ashley, a new student, arrives in a multiage first- and second-grade classroom as the students are finishing some work on place value and numeration to 99. On the basis of Ashley's transfer report, the teacher suspects Ashley has had limited experience with place value. This suspicion is strengthened after Ashley leaves a test on place value blank. The teacher decides to spend some time alone with Ashley to assess her understanding of numbers and place value. Ashley shows some understanding of numbers and is beginning to show some glimpses of understanding place value. The teacher is left wondering if she should include Ashley in the learning of an upcoming addition unit.

PREREADING ACTIVITY

Discuss what it means to understand numeration, place value, and addition. How can we tell if students really understand these concepts? How are they related to each other?

MAIN ASSESSMENT ISSUES

- Assessing students' understanding
- Responding to students' misunderstanding
- Balancing the needs of one child with the needs of the rest of the class

DISCUSSION NOTES AND QUESTIONS

Assessing Student Understanding

Ashley's Understanding of Numeration ... Ashley worked a few numeration tasks for the teacher. On the basis of the evidence, what do you think that Ashley understands about numeration and place value? What did the teacher conclude about Ashley's understanding? Do you agree with the teacher's assertion in that "she had no understanding of place value"? If Ashley were a student in your class, what questions would you ask her to assess her understanding further?

Working with Ashley ... The teacher worked with Ashley alone to determine her understanding of numeration and place value. At one point, Ashley counted out fourteen counters. The teacher asked her to make a group of ten and then make a connection between the groups and the digits 1 and 4 in the number 14. When she cannot, the teacher explained it to her. Do you agree with this strategy? If so, why? If not, what would you do differently?

NOTES FOR
"The New Student"

Responding to Student Misconceptions

Ashley had some misconceptions about number and place value. The teacher wondered what she should do to help Ashley. What strategies might a teacher use to help fix Ashley's misconceptions? What resources might teachers use to find out how to help Ashley?

Balancing the Needs of One Student

At the end, the teacher was left wondering about how to help Ashley without affecting the progress of other students. How might her other students be affected? What strategies might a teacher use to resolve this dilemma?

CONNECTIONS TO THE *PRACTICAL HANDBOOKS*

Topic	Handbook	Section
Assessing students' understanding	*K-2 Handbook*	Assessing Students' Understanding of Mathematical Concepts
	3-5 Handbook	Looking at Student Work
Responding to students' misunderstanding	*K-2 Handbook*	Assessing Students' Understanding of Mathematical Concepts
	3-5 Handbook	Looking at Students' Work
Balancing the needs of individual students	*3-5 Handbook*	Equity and Special Needs
		Managing Time and Logistics

SUGGESTIONS FOR FURTHER READING

Bright, George. "Understanding Children's Reasoning." *Teaching Children Mathematics* 3 (September 1996): 18–22.

Chappell, Michaele F., and Denisse R. Thompson. "Modifying Our Questions to Assess Students' Thinking." *Mathematics Teaching in the Middle School* 4 (April 1999): 470–74.

Jaberg, Patricia. "Assessment and Gertrude's Blanket." *Teaching Children Mathematics* 1 (April 1995): 514–17.

Moon, Jean C. "Connecting Learning and Teaching through Assessment." *Arithmetic Teacher* 41 (September 1993): 13–15.

Sullivan, Peter, and David Clarke. "Catering to All Abilities through 'Good Questions.'" *Arithmetic Teacher* 39 (October 1991): 14–18.

CHAPTER *4*

NOTES FOR
"Melanie's Place-Value Understanding"

CASE SYNOPSIS

A teacher observes the work of Melanie, a second-grade student, on place-value tasks. When Melanie's responses to place-value problems are incorrect, the teacher offers her activities that she believes will help her student. She is puzzled by what she thinks are inconsistencies in Melanie's place-value thinking and wonders how to help her student.

PREREADING ACTIVITY

Discuss different components of *place value* and what it means to "understand place value." Share common errors primary-grade students make with place-value concepts. Discuss place-value skills and concepts for second graders.

MAIN ASSESSMENT ISSUES

- Assessing one student's mathematical understanding in depth
- Using information from assessment to design instruction
- Designing an instructional program that promotes place-value concepts

DISCUSSION NOTES AND QUESTIONS

Assessing One Student's Place-Value Understanding in Depth

Melanie's Understanding of Place Value ... What were the strengths in Melanie's place-value understanding? What were the primary sources of confusion for Melanie? (With what components of place value was she having the most difficulty?) What consistencies were evident in her understanding? The teacher believed that Melanie's performance on place-value tasks was inconsistent. Do you agree? If not, what was consistent about Melanie's errors on the place-value tasks presented by the teacher? Melanie had some real misconceptions about place value. How might Melanie's misconceptions about place value have arisen?

Order of the Places ... By having her students perform tasks in which the order of hundreds, tens, and ones are rearranged, the teacher deliberately chose tasks that mix up the order of the places. Melanie did not perform well on these tasks. When is it valuable to mix up the places? How might these tasks be misleading or confusing to Melanie? What did the teacher do after seeing Melanie's performance on these tasks? What strategies did she use? What was the underlying problem Melanie had about place order? What alternative strategies might the teacher use to address this problem? The teacher had Melanie build (compose) numbers using manipulatives and base-ten blocks or stamps. What might be the role of having Melanie also decompose numbers? How might this help her place-value understanding?

NOTES FOR
"Melanie's Place-Value Understanding"

Writing Dictated Numbers ... What does having students write dictated numbers reveal about their place-value understanding? The teacher said that Melanie's errors "were different than those she had made before. Did she really not understand that numbers in the hundreds always have three digits?" What might explain Melanie's success with writing the correct number of digits on previous tasks? What might explain her confusion in writing dictated numbers?

Regrouping ... Melanie was having difficulty regrouping. What problems did she have? What might be the underlying cause of these problems? What did the teacher do when she saw Melanie's answers to the regrouping problems? What types of experiences could help Melanie understand regrouping?

Assessing Place Value Understanding ... If a student performs all the tasks in this case successfully, does that mean she understands place value? What does it mean to understand place value? How could this teacher have learned more about Melanie's place-value abilities? What other assessment strategies might she have used to uncover Melanie's thinking about place value?

Using Information from Assessment to Design Instruction

The teacher worked with Melanie after seeing her have difficulty with different place value tasks. What were the various approaches she used to work with Melanie? What types of tasks did she use to try to help her? What do you think of the ways that she addressed the weaknesses in Melanie's understanding? What types of place-value experiences could address the heart of Melanie's problems?

Designing an Instructional Program to Promote Place-Value Concepts

What are some common errors that students make when they are beginning to acquire place-value concepts? What types of instructional activities promote place-value knowledge? What do you think of this teacher's approach to teaching place value? What were her activities promoting? How might base-ten blocks or other manipulatives be used to promote key place-value concepts? What other strategies, besides the use of manipulatives, could help students learn place value?

 **CHAPTER** *4*

"Melanie's Place-Value Understanding"

CONNECTIONS TO THE *PRACTICAL HANDBOOKS*

Topic	Handbook	Section
Assessing understanding in depth	*K-2 Handbook*	Assessing Students' Understanding of Mathematical Concepts
	3-5 Handbook	Looking at Students' Work
Using assessment to design instruction	*3-5 Handbook*	Blending Instruction and Assessment
		Program Evaluation
	K–2 Handbook	Why Is It Important to Assess?
Promoting place-value understanding	*K-2 Handbook*	Assessing Students' understanding of Mathematical Concepts

SUGGESTIONS FOR FURTHER READING

Cross, Lee, and Michael Hynes. "Assessing Mathematics Learning for Students with Learning Differences." *Arithmetic Teacher* 41 (March 1994): 371–77.

Greenwood, Jonathan Jay. "On the Nature of Teaching and Assessing 'Mathematical Power' and 'Mathematical Thinking.'" *Arithmetic Teacher* 41 (November 1993): 144–52.

Jaberg, Patricia. "Assessment and Gertrude's Blanket." *Teaching Children Mathematics* 1 (April 1995): 514–17.

Sammons, Kay, Beth Kobett, Joan Heiss, and Francis (Skip) Fennell. "Linking Instruction and Assessment in the Mathematics Classroom." *Arithmetic Teacher* 39 (February 1992): 11–16.

NOTES FOR
"A Rubric Solves My Problem"

CASE SYNOPSIS

After a parent conference, an elementary school teacher is thankful that she had been carefully assessing her students' problem-solving skills. She had adapted a rubric that she received from a workshop in order to assess her students throughout the year. She wonders what the cumulative class results tell her about her teaching and her students.

PREREADING ACTIVITY

Look at the rubric in **figure 3.13** and discuss what mathematical abilities it assesses. Discuss the relative importance of each.

MAIN ASSESSMENT ISSUES

■ Adapting assessment tools to meet specific needs
■ Communicating assessment results to students and parents
■ Using assessment results to guide teaching

DISCUSSION NOTES AND QUESTIONS

Adapting Assessment Tools to Meet Specific Needs

Adapting the Rubric ... The teacher received a rubric from a colleague. After using the rubric to assess her students' problem-solving performance, she decided that it did not exactly meet her needs. What changes did she make in the rubric and why? How did the changes reflect her values about students' learning? What other changes might be made in the rubric?

Support for Changing Practices ... The teacher sought advice about her rubric from a colleague. What other ways might teachers get feedback about their assessment practices? What resources are available to help teachers change their assessment practices?

Communicating Assessment Results to Students and Parents

Communicating to Parents ... The teacher was glad that she had a rubric to explain Suzie's mathematical strengths and weaknesses to her mother. Suzie's mother seemed pleased with the explanation. In what other ways might parents react to the rubric and the explanation? What are the advantages and disadvantages of this approach? What other ways might a teacher communicate assessment results to parents?

Communicating to Students ... The teacher held the parent conference with Suzie present. What are the advantages and disadvantages of having Suzie attend the conference? In what other ways might the teacher communicate Suzie's mathematics performance to Suzie?

CHAPTER *4*

NOTES FOR
"A Rubric Solves My Problem"

Comparing Student Performance ... The parent asked the teacher to explain how Suzie's performance in mathematics compared to that of other children in class. The teacher could not respond because she had not compiled the information. If the teacher had compiled the information, how might she have responded to the parent's question? How do you respond to parents when they ask how their child compares to others in class?

Using Assessment Results to Guide Teaching

After the conference, the teacher compiled a class summary of her students' problem-solving performances based on the rubric. Look at the summary and make inferences about the students' performance and perhaps the teachers' strengths and weaknesses with regard to preparing students for problem solving. What do her students seem to do well? In what areas are they weak? What advice might you offer this teacher about subsequent lessons or activities?

CONNECTIONS TO THE *PRACTICAL HANDBOOKS*

Topic	Handbook	Section
Adapting assessment to meet specific needs	*3-5 Handbook*	Equity and Special Needs
Communicating results to others	*K-2 Handbook*	Communicating with Parents
	3-5 Handbook	Communicating with Parents
Using assessment results to guide teaching	*3-5 Handbook*	Blending Instruction and Assessment
		Program Evaluation

SUGGESTIONS FOR FURTHER READING

Brown-Herbst, Kari. "So Math Isn't Just Answers." *Mathematics Teaching in the Middle School* 4 (April 1999): 448–55.

Ensign, Jacque. "Parents, Portfolios, and Personal Mathematics." *Teaching Children Mathematics* 4 (February 1998): 346–51.

Lambdin, Diana V., and Clare Forseth. "Seamless Assessment/Instruction = Good Teaching." *Teaching Children Mathematics* 2 (January 1996): 294–98.

NOTES FOR
"Show and Tell"

CASE SYNOPSIS

A teacher asks her first- and second-grade ESL students how to share their success in mathematics with their parents. The students suggest that they make presentations to their parents. The teacher makes all the arrangements for a meeting with parents, but she wonders if she has done the right thing.

PREREADING ACTIVITY

Look at the rubric in **figure 3.20**. Discuss its strengths and weaknesses as a tool to assess students' understanding of subtraction.

MAIN ASSESSMENT ISSUES

- Communicating assessment results to parents
- Involving students in assessment
- Assessing differences in learning styles

DISCUSSION NOTES AND QUESTIONS

Communicating Assessment Results to Parents

Using Students to Communicate ... The teacher decides to let her students "show and tell" their parents what they have learned in mathematics this year. What are the advantages and disadvantages of using this approach to communicate assessment results to parents?

Communication Barriers ... Most of the parents of these students did not speak English. What strategies might a teacher of ESL students use to communicate students' performance to parents?

Involving Students in Assessment

Student Input ... The teacher actively involved her students in the assessment process—from developing rubrics to presenting results to parents. What other ways might students be involved in the assessment process? What are the advantages and disadvantages of involving students in various stages of assessment?

Student-Designed Rubrics ... The students and teacher developed a rubric to assess subtraction performance. What purpose does the rubric serve? What other criteria might be included in it? What are advantages and disadvantages in asking students to develop a rubric with the teacher?

CHAPTER *4*

NOTES FOR
"Show and Tell"

Assessing Different Learning Styles

The samples of students' work reflect different strategies. What similarities and differences in the students' work are evident?

Accommodating Learning Styles

The students' work illustrates a variety of approaches to solving subtraction problems. The teacher commented that some students wanted to work with manipulatives and others preferred not to use them. In what ways might an assessment system accommodate learning styles? What other tools or approaches might be used?

CONNECTIONS TO THE *PRACTICAL HANDBOOKS*

Topic	Handbook	Section
Communicating results to parents	K-2 Handbook	Communicating with Parents
		Student-Led Conferences
	3-5 Handbook	Communicating with Parents
Involving students in assessment	K-2 Handbook	Student-Led Conferences
	3-5 Handbook	Student Involvement and Self-Assessment
Assessing differences in learning styles	K-2 Handbook	What is the Difference between Assessment and Evaluation?
	3-5 Handbook	Equity and Special Needs

SUGGESTIONS FOR FURTHER READING

Cross, Lee, and Michael Hynes. "Assessing Mathematics Learning for Students with Learning Differences." *Arithmetic Teacher* 41 (March 1994): 371–77.

Ensign, Jacque. "Parents, Portfolios, and Personal Mathematics." *Teaching Children Mathematics* 4 (February 1998): 346–51.

Sullivan, Peter, and David Clarke. "Catering to All Abilities through 'Good Questions.'" *Arithmetic Teacher* 39 (October 1991): 14–18.

NOTES FOR
"Student-Led Conferences"

CASE SYNOPSIS

A first-grade teacher is concerned about the effectiveness of her conferences with parents and about how well students' progress and performance are communicated in these conferences. Her dissatisfaction with parent-centered conferences leads her to consider a new approach that includes students in three-way conferences. The response to this new approach is so positive that she considers another change: student-led conferences in which the students play a primary role in discussing their work. As she prepares for the upcoming conferences, she wonders how successful they will be.

PREREADING ACTIVITY

Reflect on conferences you might have had (or intend to have) with parents. How did you (or will you) share the results of students' progress? What was (will be) your purpose in sharing the results? What role, if any did (will) students play in the process? Discuss these questions as a whole group.

MAIN ASSESSMENT ISSUES

- Creating effective conferences with parents
- Encouraging students' self-assessment
- Discussing standards and expectations for performance with students

DISCUSSION NOTES AND QUESTIONS

Creating Effective Conferences with Parents

Searching for More Satisfaction ... The teacher described two different experiences in conferences with parents, using Nathan and Natasha's conferences as examples. How did these conferences differ? Why was one more satisfying to the teacher than the other? What was the teacher's purpose for having these conferences with parents? What strategies might the teacher use to improve conferences with Natasha's mother?

Bringing in the Student ... The teacher changed her assessment-reporting strategy from parent-teacher conferences to three-way conferences that included the students. What did the teacher find powerful about this model? What are advantages and disadvantages of this strategy? How might parents react to this strategy?

Student-Led Conferences ... The teacher eventually decided to change her conferences to make students the primary focus and the "leaders" of the conferences. What problems did she anticipate? What was her purpose for the new conferences? What are advantages and disadvantages of this strategy? How might parents react to this strategy?

CHAPTER *4*

"Student-Led Conferences"

Encouraging Student Self-Assessment

The teacher decided to involve students in the assessment process by asking them to assess themselves and to lead conferences with their parents. What other ways might teachers involve students in the assessment process? What factors might influence a teacher's decision to involve students in self-assessment? What are advantages and disadvantages in engaging students in the assessment process?

Discussing Standards and Expectations for Performance with Students

The teacher explained her goals and shared her expectations for performance with her students. How did she do this? How else might teachers share standards and expectations with students? What are advantages and disadvantages of sharing goals and expectations with students?

CONNECTIONS TO THE *PRACTICAL HANDBOOKS*

Topic	Handbook	Section
Creating effective conferences with parents	*K-2 Handbook*	Student-Led Conferences
	3-5 Handbook	Communicating with Parents
Encouraging students' self-assessment	*K-2 Handbook*	Student-Led Conferences
	3-5 Handbook	Student Involvement and Self-Assessment
Setting standards and expectations	*3-5 Handbook*	Defining and Using Standards in Assessment
		Making Assessment Plans

SUGGESTIONS FOR FURTHER READING

Ensign, Jacque. "Parents, Portfolios, and Personal Mathematics." *Teaching Children Mathematics* 4 (February 1998): 346–51.

Pitts, Gary O. "Breath O_2 into Your Mathematics Program—Promote Openness and Ownership." *Teaching Children Mathematics* 3 (May 1997): 496–98.

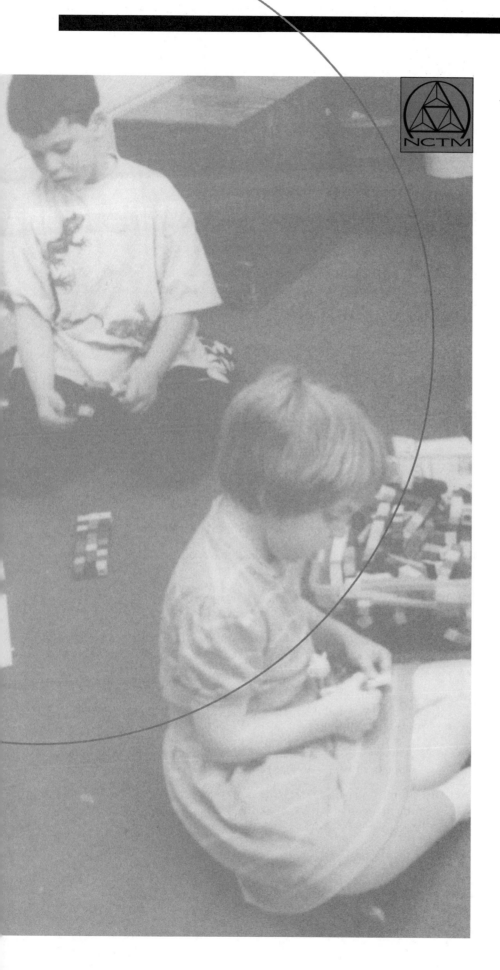

Resources

Bibliography

Bright, George. "Understanding Children's Reasoning." *Teaching Children Mathematics* 3 (September 1996): 18–22.

Brown-Herbst, Kari. "So Math Isn't Just Answers." *Mathematics Teaching in the Middle School* 4 (April 1999): 448–55.

Bryant, Deborah, and Mark Driscoll. *Exploring Classroom Assessment in Mathematics: A Guide for Professional Development.* Reston, Va.: National Council of Teachers of Mathematics, 1998.

Chappell, Michaele F., and Denisse R. Thompson. "Modifying Our Questions to Assess Students' Thinking." *Mathematics Teaching in the Middle School* 4 (April 1999): 470–74.

Clarke, David J. "Activating Assessment Alternatives in Mathematics." *Arithmetic Teacher* 39 (February 1992): 24–29.

Cole, Karen A. "Walking Around: Getting More from Informal Assessment." *Mathematics Teaching in the Middle Grades* 4 (January 1999): 224–27.

Collison, Judith. "Using Performance Assessment to Determine Mathematics Dispositions." *Arithmetic Teacher* 39 (February 1992): 40–47.

Conway, Kathleen D. "Assessing Open-Ended Problems." *Mathematics Teaching in the Middle School* 4 (May 1999): 510–14.

Cross, Lee, and Michael Hynes. "Assessing Mathematics Learning for Students with Learning Differences." *Arithmetic Teacher* 41 (March 1994): 371–77.

D'Aboy, Diana. "Assessment through Incredible Equations." *Teaching Children Mathematics* 4 (October 1997): 76–80.

Ensign, Jacque. "Parents, Portfolios, and Personal Mathematics." *Teaching Children Mathematics* 4 (February 1998): 346–51.

Glanfield, Florence, Jean Stenmark, and William S. Bush, eds. *Mathematics Assessment: A Practical Handbook for Grades K–2.* Reston, Va.: National Council of Teachers of Mathematics, forthcoming.

Greenwood, Jonathan Jay. "On the Nature of Teaching and Assessing 'Mathematical Power' and 'Mathematical Thinking.'" *Arithmetic Teacher* 41 (November 1993): 144–52.

Jaberg, Patricia. "Assessment and Gertrude's Blanket." *Teaching Children Mathematics* 1 (April 1995): 514–17.

Kroll, Diana Lambdin, Joanna O. Masingila, and Sue Tinsley Mau. "Cooperative Problem Solving: But What about Grading?" *Arithmetic Teacher* 39 (February 1992): 17–23.

RESOURCES

Lambdin, Diana V., and Clare Forseth. "Seamless Assessment/Instruction = Good Teaching." *Teaching Children Mathematics* 2 (January 1996): 294–98.

Lambdin, Diana V., and Vicki L. Walker. "Planning for Classroom Portfolio Assessment." *Arithmetic Teacher* 41 (February 1994): 318–24

Lankford, Francis G., Jr. "What Can a Teacher Learn about a Pupil's Thinking through Oral Interviews?" *Arithmetic Teacher* 40 (October 1992): 106–11.

Lindquist, Mary M. "Assessing through Questioning." *Arithmetic Teacher* 35 (January 1988): 16–18.

Long, Madeleine J., and Meir Ben-Hur. "Informing Learning through the Clinical Interview." *Arithmetic Teacher* 38 (February 1991): 44–46.

Miller, Barbara, and Ilene Kantrov. *A Guide to Facilitating Cases in Education.* Portsmouth, N.H.: Heinemann, 1998a

Miller, Barbara, and Ilene Kantrov, eds. *Casebook on School Reform.* Portsmouth, N.H.: Heinemann, 1998b.

Moon, Jean C. "Connecting Learning and Teaching through Assessment." *Arithmetic Teacher* 41 (September 1993): 13–15.

National Council of Teachers of Mathematics (NCTM). *Curriculum Standards for School Mathematics.* Reston, Va.: NCTM, 1989.

——— . *Assessment Standards for School Mathematics.* Reston, Va.: NCTM, 1995.

——— . *Principles and Standards for School Mathematics.* Reston, Va.: NCTM, 2000.

Pitts, Gay O. "Breath O_2 into Your Mathematics Program—Promote Openness and Ownership." *Teaching Children Mathematics* 3 (May 1997): 496–98.

Rowan, Thomas E., and Josepha Robles. "Using Questions to Help Children Build Mathematical Power." *Teaching Children Mathematics* 9 (May 1998): 504–509.

Sammons, Kay, Beth Kobett, Joan Heiss, and Francis (Skip) Fennell. "Linking Instruction and Assessment in the Mathematics Classroom." *Arithmetic Teacher* 39 (February 1992): 11–16.

Schoenfeld, Alan, Hugh Burkhardt, Phil Daro, Jim Ridgway, Judah Schwartz, and Sandra Wilcox. *Balanced Assessment: Elementary Grades Assessment Package 1.* White Plains, N.Y.: Dale Seymour Publications, 1999a.

——— . *Balanced Assessment: Elementary Grades Assessment Package 2.* White Plains, N.Y.: Dale Seymour Publications, 1999b.

Stenmark, Jean, ed. *Mathematics Assessment: Myths, Models, Good Questions, and Practical Suggestions.* Reston, Va.: National Council of Teachers of Mathematics, 1991.

Stenmark, Jean, and William S. Bush, eds. *Mathematics Assessment: A Practical Handbook for Grades 3–5.* Reston, Va.: National Council of Teachers of Mathematics, forthcoming.

Sullivan, Peter, and David Clarke. "Catering to All Abilities through 'Good Questions.'" *Arithmetic Teacher* 39 (October 1991): 14–18.

Swan, Malcolm. "Assessing Mathematical Processes: The English Experience." *Mathematics Teaching in the Middle School* 1 (March-April 1996): 706–11.

Tonack, De A. "A Teacher's View of Classroom Assessment: What & How." *Mathematics Teaching in the Middle School* 2 (November-December 1996): 70–78.

Wilcox, Sandra, and Perry Lanier, eds. *Using Assessment to Reshape Teaching: A Casebook for Mathematics Teachers and Teacher Educators.* Hillside, N.J.: Lawrence Erlbaum Associates, 1999.

Zawojewski, Judith. "Polishing a Data Task: Seeking Better Assessment." *Teaching Children Mathematics* 2 (February 1996): 372–78.

Index

A

acknowledgments, vi
affective issues, 9–11, 67
assessment purposes, 68–69, 71, 77
Assessment Standards for School Mathematics, vii, 2

B

beliefs, 9–11, 67, 83

C

cases
—definition, 3
—purposes, 3
—use in professional development, 4
changing practices, 14, 29, 66, 79, 90
checklists, 48–49, 57
communicating results, 47–50, 71, 90
comparing students, 52, 91
conditions for success, 29, 78
conferences, 47–50, 58, 59–61, 92, 94
criteria, 26, 30, 32, 33, 35–37, 77, 80, 82

D

documenting results, 12–13, 48–49, 69

E

expectations, 47, 70, 95

F

facilitating cases,
—guidelines, 62–64
—handling problems, 65

G

getting started, 12, 17

I

instructional decisions, 25, 40, 67, 76, 88, 91
interviewing students, 6–11, 24–25, 38–40, 41–46, 75

L

learning styles, 86, 93

M

managing time, 12–13
misconceptions, 24–25, 39–40, 41–46, 75–76, 86

N

notes, 12–13, 69

O

observations, 12–13, 41
open-ended tasks, 15, 26, 27, 28

P

parents, 13, 47–50, 52, 57–58, 90, 92, 94
peer assessment, 35
performance tasks, 15, 26, 28, 33
portfolios, 19–23, 57, 60–61, 73
Practical Handbooks 67
presentations, 33–34
prompting students, 911
POWs, 14, 24

Q

questioning, 6–11, 19
quizzes, 16, 24

R

rubrics, 20–21, 47–49, 56
—revising, 51, 90
—using, 47–49
—student developed, 21, 36, 56, 82, 92

S

scoring, 27, 30, 32, 33, 35–37, 78, 82, 83
self-assessment, 95
special needs students, 14–17, 53, 59
state-mandated assessment, 19, 72
student-led conferences, 59, 94
student thinking, 6–11, 15, 23, 29, 31, 39–40, 41–46, 53–55, 66, 75, 83
student work, 6–11, 15, 16, 22–23, 31, 34, 39–40, 41–46, 53–55

T

tasks, 21, 73
—creating, 20, 73, 79
—evaluating, 20, 73
—formating, 26
—revising, 23, 29, 73
—tests, 38,

U

understanding, 11, 29, 38–40, 41–46, 53–55, 85, 87

W

writing, 16, 19, 23, 31, 53–55